DEBATING
CHRISTIANITY

OPENING SALVOS IN THE
BATTLE WITH BELIEVERS

I0138644

JOHN W. LOFTUS

FOREWORD BY JONATHAN M.S. PEARCE
AFTERWORD BY DAVID MADISON

Trade paperback ISBN: 978-1-8382391-4-5

OB 20/36

About the author:

John W. Loftus is a philosopher and counter-apologist who earned MA, MDiv, and ThM degrees, the last of which was under William Lane Craig. John also studied in a PhD program at Marquette University. He's the *Debunking Christianity* blog owner and author of five critically acclaimed books: *Why I Became An Atheist, The Outsider Test for Faith, How to Defend the Christian Faith, Unapologetic,* and *God or Godless* (with Randal Rauser). He's also the editor of seven critically acclaimed anthologies: *The Christian Delusion, The End of Christianity, Christianity is Not Great, Christianity in the Light of Science, The Case against Miracles, Varieties of Jesus Mythicism,* and *God and Horrendous Suffering.*

A note about the book:

This book is a collection of debate openers, together with a few added chapters, that hopes to provide a springboard to further reading. All of the subjects are covered in my previous collections and books. Though there might be some superficial editing of these debate openers to fit the remit of this book, none of the content has been substantially changed from the original debates.

Praise for the books of John W. Loftus:

I read every single one of your books leading up to our multiple debates on various different topics. They are elite level and the Audible editions are must owns. They go beyond the surface level pop atheist arguments that are easily dismissed and require deep exegetical and historical research. Anyone that hasn't read/doesn't own your stuff, are missing out massively.

As a Catholic apologist, I cannot recommend this book [*How To Defend the Christian Faith*] enough. The arguments therein are elite level arguments that ANY believer MUST answer if they are to defend their faith against the very best that atheism has to offer. I own this book and give copies out frequently. I also own it on Audible. I should have left a 5 star review a long time ago. I just left a 5 star review now.

> – William Albrecht, Christian apologist, author of *The Secret History of Transubstantiation: Pulling Back The Veil On The Eucharist*

Every John W. Loftus book is a must-read; he continues to assemble some of the finest and most insightful minds in contemporary counter-apologetics. Putting biblical miracle claims under the magnifying lens, it weighs the evidence and finds them wanting. The Case against Miracles is a superb resource and a handy field guide for anyone forced to traipse through the treacherous jungles of the miraculous.

> – David Fitzgerald, author of *Nailed, Jesus: Mything in Action*, and *The Complete Heretic's Guide to Western Religion* series

The previous four Loftus anthologies have left little of Christianity intact. Of course, apologists continue to flail, but the case against miracles–so massively documented in this new 562-page book–wipes out all vestiges of this primitive, magical thinking.

> – Dr. David Madison, author of *Ten Tough Problems in Christian Thought and Belief*

In 2008, John W. Loftus launched what would become a definitive series of anti-apologetic works. The Case against Miracles is the capstone volume of this astonishing output, and it's an impressive achievement. Any thoughtful Christian whose conviction rests on the evidence of miracles who reads this book with an open mind will be hard pressed not to abandon--or at least profoundly rethink--his or her beliefs. Of course, true believers seldom approach works critical of their faiths with an open mind, which is why The Case against Miracles will probably be of greater value to secular students of religion and especially to those drawn to the challenges of anti-apologetics.

- Tom Flynn, the late former Senior Editor of *Free Inquiry* magazine

I'm not sure there is anyone out there right now who articulates atheistic augments as well as John Loftus does, and this book on horrendous suffering is no exception. In it Loftus has done a great job in marshaling a stellar group of scholars in offering one of the best attempts at criticizing the Christian faith in a more comprehensive way with regard to the problem of evil. Believers who hold to a theistic perspective should seriously--and more deeply--study the alternative perspectives and questions that this anthology poses for theism. They should especially be more mindful of these kinds of criticisms when speaking with people who do not believe like we do that the Christian God is so good.

- Dr. David Geisler, President Norm Geisler International Ministries, and Adjunct Professor, Southern Evangelical Seminary and Veritas International University.

Other books by John Loftus:

Why I Became an Atheist

The Christian Delusion (ed.)

The End of Christianity (ed.)

The Outsider Test for Faith: How to Know Which Religion Is True

God or Godless?: One Atheist. One Christian. Twenty Controversial Questions (With Randal Rauser)

Christianity Is Not Great: How Faith Fails (ed.)

How to Defend the Christian Faith: Advice from an Atheist

Christianity in the Light of Science: Critically Examining the World's Largest Religion (ed.)

UnApologetic: Why Philosophy of Religion Must End

The Case against Miracles (ed.)

God and Horrendous Suffering (ed.)

Varieties of Jesus Mythicism: Did He Even Exist? (With Robert M. Price, eds.)

Contents

*It has been a lonely adventure doing what I
have done for about two decades so far.
I have spent a massive amount of time on computers
and phones, with my nose inside books and articles, while watching pod-
casts and videos, sometimes at the same time!
I couldn't have done this without a lot of encouragement.
So I dedicate this book to the people who encouraged me
throughout the years, especially Jonathan Pearce.
He recommended my works, wrote posts on my blog,
two chapters for my books, then initiated and put together this particular
book. He is a good man who is an extremely valuable indefatigable advocate for reason and science.*

Foreword

The Debate Is Over, and Has Been for a Long Time

By Jonathan M.S. Pearce

I have a lot to thank John Loftus for since he allowed me to write at his blog home (*Debunking Christianity*) for some time in my early days of writing and grappling with the big philosophical ideas of God or not God. The answer, even then, seemed blatantly obvious: not God.

Now, many years later, the answer is as blatant and as obvious as ever it was. Indeed, I look at some of the claims that theists make, or at least *accept* in the Bible, for example, and shake my head. I ask them (either in person or in my mind): "Do you seriously believe...?"

The end of that question has so many variations and none of them bode well for the Christian. Do you seriously believe that...

...God flooded the entire world and killed everyone on it bar eight, and countless animals, because he got his design wrong?

...people lived to almost a thousand years old?

...giants – the Nephilim – lived before and after the flood?

...God actually teleported people?

...the moon and the sun stood still?

...dead zombie saints paraded around Jerusalem for everyone to see?

...a donkey and a snake talked?

...an army was raised from bones?

...a man lived inside a whale for days?

...God killed all the firstborn *children* of the entire Egyptian nation because the Pharaoh said no (especially given that God had hardened his heart anyway)?

And so on.

I mean, do you *really believe* that? Oh, yes? Really? *Really?*

It's hard to get past the idea that otherwise intelligent people who require so much evidence to believe in evolution or cosmology or some other well-defended claim believe *these* such claims on incredibly low evidential thresholds. The Bible is largely mythological and the nuggets of truth that may or may not be contained within are so overlaid with embellishment as to effectively be myth.

Yet so many people cling onto this belief. They still cling on despite the result being in. They build their world around this belief. They vote in ways supported by or supporting this belief. They moralize on account of this belief.

And that can be dangerous.

We should be living in a post-God world but some people are willfully slow at catching on.

So work still remains to be done to convince these believers out of their worldview. As they say, unfortunately, you cannot rationalize someone out of a position that they never rationalized themselves into.

Belief is, invariably, psychological. Rational arguments are smart little add-ons, post hoc additions to positions already taken, and rarely bedrocks upon which people build frameworks toward a conclusion. Essentially, and this seems particularly the case for Christians, believers start with a conclusion (the truth of the Bible) and spend their lives scrabbling around looking for the foundations.

But the belief is a castle in the air. The foundations are nowhere to be seen.

But where deconversion often has a psychological trigger, there is still a need for presenting cogent arguments and providing ammunition for counter-apologists and skeptics. Books like this and all of Loftus's previous works provide fertile ground from which seeds of doubt can find nourishment and growth. Content like this acts as the storehouses of nourishment for skeptics and doubters giving them a balanced diet for a healthy worldview.

John Loftus has contributed about as much as any other writer out there to showing that the Christian does not have a rational foundation to their belief. He has pulled back the curtain to exhibit the trickery. He has presented an impressive array of fantastic expertise in his various

2

anthologies. He has collected together authors to write on every topic you could hope to read in the domain of counter-apologetics, philosophy and theology, history, archaeology and exegesis, that shows there is really no good reason left to believe in God and, more particularly, the Christian iteration thereof.

His back catalog of titles is all you ever need to read to be entirely confident that atheism is a far more reasonable conclusion than Christian theism. And that's some accomplishment. Add to his published works the content of his that you can find online at his blog *Debunking Christianity*, and you realize that Loftus's contributions are impressively voluminous.

Public debates, unlike writing a book to present a case, are not really about the content, about the arguments as logical constructions or watertight cases or persuasive ideas. They are about constructing a persuasive argument and winning on account of rhetoric and polished technique.

However, while at the events the rhetorical flourishes are the more memorable moments that carry significant weight, it really is only veneer-thick. The debater still needs to cover the hard yards of piecing together a coherent case to present good content.

Loftus has debated a number of opponents on various subjects, and when you read his debate openers, as they are presented here, it is hard to disagree with the conclusions that they lead him toward. Stripped back from rhetoric and on-the-night performance, these debate openers as arguments are full of great content.

There is a wide range of topic areas covered here, too. It is something of a "DVD Extras" style of book, though that reference is probably dated in an age of streaming. A book like this is the icing on the cake of everything else that Loftus has written and provides a great starting point to launch into further research on these different topics: the existence of God, Jesus' birth and resurrection, faith, atheism, epistemology, suffering and genocide. Big subjects about which Loftus has written in great depth elsewhere. But this is as good a place to start as anywhere.

Jonathan M.S. Pearce, author of *30 Arguments Against God* and *Why I Am Atheist and Not a* Theist; columnist and feature writer at the nonreligious media platform *OnlySky*.

3

Preface

My critiques of the Christian faith mainly focus on the lack of sufficient objective evidence for its claims. The requirement of sufficient evidence for any given culturally indoctrinated faith is something that my book, *The Outsider Test for Faith,* goads believers into demanding of their faiths. Believers should require of their own faith what they require of the other faiths they reject, with no double-standards. In my book, *How to Defend the Christian Faith: Advice from an Atheist,* I show Christians and apologists how to think about their faith and the evidence. I argue—with tongue-in-cheek—that if they were consistent, and honest with the lack of evidence, they wouldn't be apologists at all. This same lack of sufficient evidence is why reasoning with Christian philosophers about unevidenced beliefs is largely a fool's errand, as I wrote about in my book, *Unapologetic: Why Philosophy of Religion Must End*. My critiques of the Christian faith won't change no matter which philosophical theology is fashionable.

My critiques revolve around the following five reasons not to believe.

1. The Bible. It debunks itself. It contains forgeries, borrowed pagan myths, and is inconsistent within itself. It tells a plethora of ancient superstitious tales that lack direct evidence for them that don't make any sense at all. It has a god that evolved from a polytheistic one who lives in the sky above the earth, who does both good and bad, who makes room for both angels and demons and thinks a god/human blood sacrifice can magically ransom us from the grip of the devil (the first widely accepted atonement theory). For this case see the latter half of my book, *Why I Became an Atheist,* and several other anthologies, including *The Christian Delusion*, and *The End of Christianity,*

2. The Church. It's supposed to be an institution of God's people, who claim they are the only ones who have God the Holy Spirit inside them who informs them of the truth, teaches them what is good, and empowers them to do good deeds. Yet we see no objective evidence on behalf of this and plenty of disconfirming evidence against it. Their first mistake was to choose the currently accepted canonized texts of the Bible, which in addition to reason #1 above, contain many barbaric texts which should be rejected by all civilized people. Where was the Holy Spirit when they choose those barbaric texts? The only excuse for the church of today is that they do not read the Bible. Ignorance is bliss they say. The history of the church and of the people claiming to have God the Holy Spirit inside them reveals a continuous spectacle of atrocities, such that its history is a damning indictment upon the god they profess to believe. Why can't God do any better than that? Contrary to their empty rhetoric that atheists live as though their God exists, believers live as though *their God doesn't exist*. But when they actually do read their Bible and follow its barbaric morality it's additionally clear that *their god doesn't exist*. Either way their god doesn't exist. Get it? For this case see my anthology, *Christianity is Not Great*.

3. There is no direct evidence for any of its miracles. For this case, see my anthology, *The Case against Miracles*.

4. Science. Science is answering the very mysteries that produce religious belief in the first place. The fewer mysteries we have in the world then the less we feel the need to believe. Furthermore, when we put Christianity under the microscope of science, as we do in my anthology, *Christianity in Light of Science*, Christianity doesn't survive.

5. The problem of horrendous suffering. This is evidence is as close to a refutation of an all-powerful, all-knowing and all-loving god concept as is possible. For this case, see my anthology, *God and Horrendous Suffering*.

The lack of evidence for Christianity, along with the amount of evidence that undercuts it, renders any claim of it being true as delusional.

Introduction: I'm Not an Angry Atheist

I am not an angry atheist. I have nothing to be angry about. If I have ever shown anger, it's because I was responding to what I considered to be willful ignorance, idiocy and/or attempts to belittle me.

If we are angry, Christians will see this as a sign we are "God haters." Christians are looking for psychological reasons for why we don't believe, because many of them don't think we reject their faith on intellectual grounds. They believe we reject the Christian faith on emotional or psychological grounds. R.C. Sproul's book, *If There's a God, Why Are There Atheists?*, is typical of this kind of thinking. Sproul claims that the nature of God is "repugnant" to human beings. We want to be our own authority, and we refuse to acknowledge our sins before a holy God."

I deny this explains why I don't believe. I just don't think the Christian God exists. I am not a God hater. How can I hate God if God doesn't exist? How can I hate someone like Jesus, whom I have never met in person?

To better understand us, the Christian merely needs to ask herself what she thinks about Islam. Do you hate Allah? Are you angry with Allah? Do you refuse to acknowledge his authority in your life? Are you in rebellion against him?

The point is that these kinds of questions are silly, aren't they? They are silly because Christians do not believe Allah exists (though there are some theologians who claim adherents of both religions are really praying to the same god). They do not consider themselves in rebellion against Allah. They are not Allah haters, either. They just don't believe he exists.

That's us, when it comes to the Christian God. We just don't think he exists. We don't consider ourselves to be rebelling against him, just as you don't consider yourself to be rebelling against Allah.

Let's go a little deeper.

Let's say we are angry ex-Christians (again, I am not). What would we be angry about? Some of us might be angry for "wasting" a good portion of our lives on something that we finally concluded was a delusion. Christian, let's say this described you in a few years. How would you feel about it, when you could've been doing something different with your life? That may describe some of us. The time, effort and money we spent on this Christian delusion was simply "wasted." (I, however, don't think anything we do for other people, or any learning we do is ever wasted). We might be angry simply because we felt duped.

We might be angry at how we were treated by church people. We could tell plenty of stories about abuse and mistreatment at the hands of leaders in the church who hid behind the cloak of the Bible. People who have left the Catholic Church because of molester-priests and the subsequent cover-up, have a right to be angry, correct? Then there are Muslims who are angry because other Muslims blow up their children while walking to school. We too may have been abused by church people in some different, milder ways, but it is abuse just the same. And if we are angry about it, we have a right to be angry.

There are other reasons to be angry. We could be angry for the way religion is forced upon us by the majority through the law and upheld in court cases. We could be angry at what Richard Dawkins describes as child-abuse in the form of indoctrinating children to believe. We could be angry with how our tax money is being used to support churches, or that churches don't have to pay taxes. We could simply be angry at ignorance parading itself as education, or angry at the inhibiting of science because of religious based beliefs and fears.

Whether we're angry or not says nothing about whether Christianity is true. If what we believe is correct, then we have a right to be somewhat angry for being taught a delusion.

Besides, I see a great deal of anger coming from the Christian community. According to many sermons preached in America every Sunday we are evil doers, God haters, tools of Satan, and unworthy of any kindness at all, for we're already headed to hell. I have personally been viciously verbally attacked for arguing against Christianity. If Christianity wins in the market-place of ideas, why should Christians be angry with me? Let the truth prevail. In a prior era, Christians would have burned me at the stake for being an evil doer. And I was serious when I said I think some of these Christians who have personally maligned me would've lit the fires!

The reason for anger on both sides of this great debate is because we're in a cultural war of values over the hearts and minds of people, especially the children. But we're simply not angry at God at all. We might be angry with ourselves, those who led us to believe in the first place, church people who abused us, and so on. But we're not angry with God. We don't believe the Christian God exists.

The question you might ask me as a reader, and particularly as a believer, might be, "Why are you doing this? All of this?"

In fact, many years ago, a blogger named WarrenL asked me some pointed questions about why I'm debunking Christianity. He started with the following two questions:

WL: "As I understand it you spent a good portion of your life assenting to Christianity and now with your book and regular articles it appears you plan to spend a good portion of it debunking Christianity. (1) What is your motivation for this? (2) It seems that religion will always be a part of our culture. Do you see any good or value in Christianity?"

Question #1: My motivation for debunking Christianity on the web is pretty much the same as any Christian apologist, except I don't do it to glorify God, and I'm not taking anyone to heaven with me. Christian apologists want to know that their beliefs are true, and one good way to do that is to get in the ring and argue for them. In doing so, they learn things and find better arguments to defend what they believe. This describes me too. Some want to make a name for themselves, some want the satisfaction of winning an intellectual contest (the competitive urge), while others want to gain some respect from their perceived peers, and still others promote themselves to make some money off what they write. So the motivations of us all are multifaceted.

I personally like an intellectual challenge. Can I describe what I believe in a way that makes some sense to those who disagree? That's quite a challenge, and I like to try since our control beliefs are so diametrically opposed to each other.

I am a teacher. Since I've spent a great part of my life being educated about Christianity why not use what I've learned and not waste it? As a teacher I'm against people believing in wrongheaded Christian ideas that I tend to think are based upon ignorance, although that's the stuff that maddens me, since many apologists don't seem ignorant at all! What is it, I ask myself, that makes us believe different things where each side has this strong tendency to think the other side is just plain ignorant? This is where discussing and debating these things intrigues me to the utmost, and so I try again to explain why I see things differently. In the process I get a better glimpse of what it takes to cross that great divide between us, and I test my

9

own explanations of why I see things the way I do. How can we each be so sure the other is wrong? That intrigues me like nothing else I know.

I also believe that life is better from my perspective, having been a former Christian myself. I can be more...well...human. Church people are stuffy people who are so judgmental. I only realized how much this is true after leaving, although I thought it was true while still in the church. There is a life to be lived to the fullest, and Christians are afraid to do this. I love the freedom to live like I want to without the fear of hell or the judgment of other Christians.

Don't get me wrong here, I still am every bit the honest and good person I was before (without the so-called help of the Holy Spirit), but I no longer feel guilty for what I think about, whereas Christians always seem to struggle with thoughts of hate, greed, lust, and the like. I only have to be concerned with what I actually do, not what I think about. I no longer have to give of my hard-earned money to fund a church building in hopes God will multiply it back to me. I don't have to worry about what Ms. Peabody thinks if I go play pool at the bars, and I no longer have to waste so much of my time attending church, reading the Bible, praying, and evangelizing. I no longer have the overwhelming guilt when I failed in these tasks, either, nor do I need to confess my failures in these tasks with tears in my eyes to God. If I see a pretty girl, I can imagine what she looks like naked if I want to (I am after all, a male), so long as I do nothing about it, since I'm a very happily married man. I can drink and get buzzed if I want to. If someone does get in my face, I don't have to be a mild-mannered man, but I can tell him to get the hell away from me, and I can say it like I mean it. I can waste away my time watching TV without guilt if I want to. I can drive over the speed limit if I want to without fear of God's judgment, although I don't speed hardly ever. I also love the freedom to think for myself without feeling like I must justify everything I believe in the Bible (have you recently tried to come up with a view of hell from the Bible that passes the moral test?).

And I love the fact that my thinking is not hamstrung by fear of being cast into hell, because I'm a freethinker. I also love being good to people just because I want to, and not because I have to, and I am. Even as an atheist, I have solid reasons to be good without God.

I want to help people who are struggling with their Christian faith to know there are others out there like me. As I was thinking my way out of Christianity I did it alone with my books. I read things. Then I thought about

10

them. And I read some other things. But I struggled, and struggled. I only sought to talk to a very select few people about my doubts, because most all of the people I knew were Christians, and I didn't want to be branded as a heretic, or shunned, nor did I want to create doubt in anyone else, since I wasn't sure what I would end up believing at the end of the tunnel, so to speak. So my books and my blog are to help people discuss these things. It's to let them know there is light at the end of the tunnel, and that others like me have come out of the tunnel and we're okay. It's okay to doubt. You'll be fine. In fact, I believe it's better over here.

I believe there are inherent dangers with religious beliefs. They don't always materialize, but they do have their impact in various ways. There are political reasons, which I don't touch on much at all. There is a large voting block of evangelical Christians in America that help elect our local and state and national governmental officials. This large block of evangelical Christians also participate in letter campaigns to change public policy in ways I don't approve of. Atheists generally think Christian theism inhibits scientific progress, creates class struggles, sexism, homophobia, racism, mass neurosis, intolerance and environmental disasters. There are some dispensationalist Christians in America who believe the Jews are somehow still in God's plan. So they defend Israel no matter what they do, which fans the flames of war between the militant Muslims and the US.

Finally, listen to Robert W. Funk and Robert M. Price's motivations for debunking Christianity. Robert W. Funk in his book, *Honest to Jesus,* wrote:[1]

> As I look around me, I am distressed by those who are enslaved by a Christ imposed upon them by a narrow and rigid legacy. There are millions of Americans who are the victims of a mythical Jesus conjured up by modern evangelists to whip their followers into a frenzy of guilt and remorse—and cash contributions. I agonize over their slavery in contrast to my freedom. I have a residual hankering to free my fellow human beings from this bondage. Liberation from fear and ignorance is always a worthy cause. In the last analysis, however, it is because I occasionally glimpse an unknown Jesus lurking in and behind Christian legend and piety that I persist in my efforts to find my way through the mythical and

---

[1] Funk, Robert W.(1996), *Honest to Jesus: Jesus for a New Millennium*, San Francisco: Harper-Collins, p. 19.

11

legendary debris of the Christian tradition. And it is the lure of this glimpse that I detect in other questers and that I share with them.

Robert M. Price wrote this:[1]

>We are viewed as insidious villains seeking to undermine the belief of the faithful, trying to push them off the heavenly path and into Satan's arms. But this is not how we view ourselves at all. We find ourselves entering the field as the champions and zealots for a straightforward and accurate understanding of the Bible as an ancient text. In our opinion, it is the fundamentalist, the apologist for Christian supernaturalism, who is propagating false and misleading views of the Bible among the general populace. We are not content to know better and to shake our heads at the foolishness of the untutored masses. We want the Bible to be appreciated for what it is, not for what it is not. And it is not a supernatural oracle book filled with infallible dogmas and wild tales that must be believed at the risk of eternal peril.

As far as the second question of WarrenL goes, yes I do see some good in Christianity. It has saved marriages headed for divorce (although it can create an oppressive family structure where the wife is dominated and must obey her husband). It has changed rebellious teenagers who were hell bent on doing drugs, sex, and crime (but there are other down-to-earth reasons why they should change). It offers a heavenly comfort (even if it is a false one) in believing that God can help Christians and will bring them to heaven (although it also requires believing that our neighbors, friends, mother, father, siblings, and cousins might spend forever in hell).

No one argues that Christian believers don't do some good humanitarian deeds in the name of their Christ. They do. But the good deeds done are good precisely because they are based on humanitarian and/or trans-humanitarian values. In other words, if it's a morally good deed then nobody needs a religion to do that deed. This point was made by Christopher Hitchens, who repeatedly stumped believers by asking them to come up with one moral action they could do that nonbelievers could not also do.

The problem however, is that horrific deeds are sometimes morally justified by good people because of a faith-based religion. Steven Weinberg

---

[1] Price in Price, Robert M. & Lowder, Jeffery Jay (2005), *The Empty Tomb: Jesus Beyond the Grave*, Amherst, Prometheus, p. 15.

is quoted as making this point: "With or without religion, good people can behave well and bad people can do evil; but for good people to do evil—that takes religion." (Steven Weinberg, *The Federal*). If readers want a complete picture of the deeds of Christians, then seriously consider the many morally atrocious deeds their faith-based morals have caused. Christianity is red with blood in tooth and in claw, as documented in my anthology "Christianity is not Great." Throughout most of its history violence was its theme, its program, and its method for converting people and keeping believers in the fold. Its history is a history of violence. There is no escaping this. Liberal scholar Charles Kimball admits this much: "A strong case can be made that the history of Christianity contains considerably more violence and destruction than that of most other major religions."[1]

Christians have a false and irrational hope, but just don't know it. They are simply deluded into thinking their lives have some grand ultimate purpose. So who's better off? Someone who lives a life of delusion, doing things because they think it will matter for eternity, along with the daily guilt for not having lived up to those standards, or someone who lives with his or her feet planted squarely on the ground with the only reality that is to be had?

As far as the answer to the earlier Question #2 ("Do you see any good or value in Christianity?"), the following chapters will go some way to giving the reader something to think about.

– John Loftus, adapted from some earlier 2008 writing.

[11] (Kimball, Charles (2002)m *When Religion Becomes Evil*, San Francisco: HarperSanFrancisco, p. 27.

PART 1: THE OPENING SALVOS

1 – My Inaugural Speech on the State of the Case for Christianity

This was originally written in 2013 for my blog audience, which is now updated for this collection.

Over the years I have written other summaries of my case against Christianity. The first one was based on my magnum opus, *Why I Became an Atheist*. It was written in 2008 called "Why I Am Not a Christian: A Summary of My Case Against Christianity" published by The SecularWeb.[1] The second one is found in my anthology, *The End of Christianity*, in a chapter titled "Christianity is Wildly Improbable" in 2011 (pp. 75-104). The third one is found in chapter 9 of my book *The Outsider Test for Faith* in 2013, titled "Debating Christianity Based on the Test" (pp.171-205). The fourth one can be found in a chapter for my book, *How To Defend the Christian Faith: Advice from an Atheist*, that summarizes the kind of arguments wannabe apologists should be forewarned about in their quest to be apologists. It's titled "Realize in Advance the Monumental Challenges" (pp. 39-51). My latest summary is found in my anthology, *God and Horrendous Suffering*, which has nearly 15 thousand words in it. It's called, "In Defense of Hitchens's Razor" (pp. 17-49). I make two main points in it: 1) The Christian faith has no objective evidence on its behalf, and 2) The Christian faith makes no sense at all. None of my summaries stress the same exact things. But they seem to keep getting better and better.

Ladies and gentlemen, dignitaries and non-dignitaries, believers and non-believers, I am honored to briefly speak to you tonight on the inaugural of

---

[1] Loftus, John W. (2008), "Why I Am Not a Christian: A Summary of My Case Against Christianity," *The Secular Web*, https://infidels.org/library/modern/john-loftus-christianity/ (Accessed 05/12/2022).

my next year's term as president and owner of my blog. In about 2006, I started my blog. Each year, you have re-elected me to another term. I have posted something about 1.5 times a day ever since. I have fought many battles with both believers and nonbelievers in order to stay on track with my goal of debunking Christianity in all of its forms. It has been very time consuming but very rewarding work. You already know my goals and what I have to offer, and you also know I have critics on both sides of these debates, but you still re-elected me for yet another term at *Debunking Christianity* [DC], for which I am very grateful.

So my heartfelt thanks goes out to the various writers who have been team members at DC over the years, most notably the late, great Hector Avalos, and including Harry McCall, Jonathan M.S. Pearce, Franz Keikeben, Richard C. Miller, and David Madison. Thanks also to my readers for the many years of comments and debate. You have helped to make the blog one of the top places to discuss the best arguments for and against Christianity. This means a great deal to me personally. Without you, I would have thrown in the towel a long time ago out of fatigue, discouragement and/or financial ruin.

As to the state of the case for Christianity, it's abysmal.

It has no more epistemic warrant for it than any other religion. Of that, I am sure. The only people who don't see this for what it is are deluded, indoctrinated, enculturated and even brainwashed Christians. This goes for the highly educated as well as the Bible thumping ignoramuses. This goes for the conservatives as well as for the moderates and liberals.

Religious faith is a cognitive bias that overestimates the force of confirming evidence and underestimates the force of disconfirming evidence.

Faith ignores the probabilities at every turn in favor of what believers prefer to be true. Faith itself is irrational and dangerous. We should think exclusively in terms of the probabilities when it comes to matters of truth propositions about the nature and existence of the universe and our place in it.

Typically, whenever I say such things, believers of all persuasions will pounce on me, arguing that it is improbable the universe even exists, much less the complexity of the human brain and self-consciousness. What they fail to understand is that this is not thinking exclusively in terms of probabilities after all, even though it sounds that way. For to think

16

exclusively in terms of probabilities means comparing the likelihood of the naturalistic hypothesis with the many others. The question is not whether it is improbable for this universe to exist as we find it. The question is whether one out of the thousands of god-hypotheses are more probable than the natural explanation.

Likewise, the question isn't whether natural explanations of the so-called "Easter Event" are improbable. The question is whether those natural explanations are more improbable than that a man lived after being dead for three days in the ancient past, an impossible event within the natural order on its own. Not even other non-Christian religious believers think the evidence for the resurrection is good enough to become Christians, even the millions of Jews who believed in Yahweh and miracles and prophecy in the days of Jesus! LET. THIS. SINK. IN. *That's* thinking in terms of the probabilities and they can best be understood if we become Bayesians in our thinking (you can do it without the math).

Believers utterly fail to understand the difference between science-based reasoning and faith-based reasoning. Believers cannot possibly be intellectually honest when pointing out that science has its flaws as an excuse for their faith. To think exclusively in terms of probabilities means pitting these two methods for attaining truth against each other in order to determine which one produces knowledge, faith or science, belief or reason. But we know that faith solves nothing. It has no method for settling disputes. Faith cannot make anything true that isn't true. It adds nothing for a person of faith to say, for instance, "I believe a flipped quarter will turn up heads." It either will or it won't. Faith adds nothing to the probabilities at all.

Likewise, the same goes for a god, a religion, or a miracle. Faith is superfluous, irrelevant, and based on improbabilities. It is irrational and even dangerous. Compared with faith, science is the only game in town. It is the only way to even determine the probabilities, that is, science in its broadest terms, which includes sense data and personal experiences. The very fact that some apologists have argued against thinking exclusively in terms of probabilities and science should be a red-light warning that the case for their faith is abysmal.

All Christians have as the basis for their faith are private subjective experiences and testimonies from pre-scientific superstitious people in the first century who had private subjective experiences, and that's it. *That's it!* There is no objective evidence for anything specific to their faith at all. All of the so-called "objective evidence" is nothing more than private subjective experiences to the core. Based on these experiences, we find a whole host of believers who have been so convinced of them that they have repeatedly lied about their faith,[1] which has destroyed any credibility it could have had in the first place. There is therefore no reason to believe it even if it's true! LET. THIS. SINK. IN.

Given this state of affairs I have come to two conclusions.

First, I have little patience for atheists who want to have a discussion for discussion's sake, or who want to play the devil's advocate. The case is closed, slammed shut by the overwhelming evidence. So nitpicking about this or that argument, as if they matter to the case as a whole, is like helping to rearranging chairs on the Titanic, which is doomed to go down into the deep. Why bother doing this? I would no more spend time arguing against an ineffective atheist argument than I would spend time baking cookies I had no intention of doing anything with. It's a waste of my time given the overall case against Christianity and faith, along with its dangers. I will, however, argue against ineffective self-serving approaches taken by other atheists, as I have done.

Second, given the abysmal state of the case for Christianity I have reason to ridicule it. Christians don't like it, I know. They want me to take their faith seriously. The fact is that I have done so, repeatedly. But after studying it for over 40 years my informed conclusion is that it is a delusion, through and through. Christians are brainwashed to believe. There is no reason at all to believe it. Only children in their thinking continue doing so. I have also produced the arguments and the evidence. There isn't anything left for me to consider. So I have earned the right to ridicule Christianity and its defenders, and I do. For any atheists who think this is inappropriate, let me remind them that, for centuries, Christians ridiculed skeptics into silence (and killed us). It marginalized us. People were led by this ridicule to think skeptics were evil people, and they still do. We all ridicule views we think have no basis in truth. Everyone who is not a Scientologist ridicules this religion, as we do Fred Phelps of the Westboro Baptist Church, and Pat Robertson. We do this with all dead gods and religions too.

---

[1] See my piece: Loftus, John W. (2012), "Christians Are Not Credible Witnesses So Christianity is Not Credible Either," *Debunking Christianity*, https://www.debunking-christianity.com/2012/11/christians-are-not-credible-witnesses.html, (Accessed 04/20/2022).

What happens to religions is that eventually they die. In fact, many different Christianities have already died out. Christians claim that skeptics have come and gone but their faith has withstood all attacks so far and survived.

The truth, however, is much, much different.

The Christianities that have survived into the present are newly invented ones coming as the result of skeptical attacks, sometimes coming from within, and as they came into contact with other cultures. This process happens in each generation. Just think of the modernist rift due to the enlightenment, which divided all denominations to some degree. This division can be attributed to the skeptical attacks of Hume, Kant, Darwin, Nietzsche, Paine, Ingersoll, and many others. The liberal church is a testament to the effectiveness of the skeptical arguments. Even within conservative denominations there are liberal ideas that would have been condemned by the Office of the Inquisition, like Open Theism, a metaphorical and/or annihilation view of Hell, women in leadership, Preterism, the emergent church, acceptance of a gay orientation, the mythical (or literary) view of Genesis 1-2, and so forth and so on.

I have lived long enough to see this theological drift in which evangelicals now embrace what only a few decades ago they rejected, Neo-Orthodoxy.[1] The Christianities practiced and believed by any denomination today are not something the early church would recognize as orthodoxy. And the future church will be almost as different.

Let's have done then with this cockamamie notion that the church has survived our attacks. No it hasn't. In each generation the former Christianities die out, so to speak, and new ones are invented.

But eventually Christianity itself as a whole will die out. We know this. As it dies out and as people become more aware that the case is as bad as I say it is, people will ridicule it more and more. It's already happening across the internet. Eventually people will ridicule it just as we do to the other dead gods and religions. So complain all you want to. It deserves to be ridiculed just as the child in the story did to the emperor who had no clothes on. Hey, you're naked! No, you really, really are!

---

[1] See my piece: Loftus, John W. (2012), "The New Evangelical Orthodoxy, Relativism, and the Amnesia of It All," *Debunking Christianity*, https://www.debunking-christianity.com/2012/12/the-new-evangelical-orthodoxy.html, (Accessed 04/20/2022).

This doesn't mean I won't continue making my case respectfully against Christians, but I have earned the right to ridicule it whenever I do, and I will. It deserves it.

In closing I wish you all well. This isn't personal with me. I'm not angry. The reason you think I am is because by me arguing against your faith, you take it personally. The reason you do is because you think your God agrees with you about everything;[1] because you create your own God in your own image, and your own religion with your own gospel. I am no angrier with your god than I am angry with any of the other gods.

Thanks for reading. It should be another turbulent year. That is, if I have the stamina and stomach for continuing to argue against a religion I consider has no more epistemic warrant than the religions of Ra, Marduk, Baal, Zeus, Poseidon, Apollo, Thor, or Odin in their days.

But as the Bud Light commercial says, "Here we go!"

---

[1] See Yong, Ed (2009), "Creating God in one's own image," *Discover Magazine*, https://www.discovermagazine.com/planet-earth/creating-god-in-ones-own-image, (Accessed 04/20/2022).

2 – The Existence of God: Loftus vs David Wood

No one would value the opinion of any judge who had a double standard, one for the plaintiff, and a different one for the defendant. Any judge who did that would be placing his thumb on the scales of justice. He wouldn't be weighing the evidence fairly. And we would object to his ruling. All of us.

Tonight, I'm going to argue that this is what Christian apologists do when it comes to the evidence for their God. I'm going to talk about eight of their double standards. My challenge to David will be to explain why he has them. I intend to force him to consistently apply the same standards across the board for his faith claims.

I'm going to start out by granting that a minimal god of some kind might possibly exist. Almost every atheist including Richard Dawkins and Victor Stenger admit this possibility. We just think it's very improbable. Especially improbable is the kind of God in which evangelicals believe. This is the God I'll focus on tonight. That God does not exist.

The first double standard is that David holds other god-hypotheses to a much higher standard than his own. Even if David can successfully show that our universe began to exist and that it's consistent with his belief in a creator God, or even if he can defend some of the classical arguments for God's existence, so what? All he's done is to show that these things are consistent with his faith. But just showing that they are consistent with his faith does not show that his faith is probable. For they are also consistent with a god who created this world as nothing more than a scientific experiment who thinks of us as rats in a maze, wondering what we will conclude about it all and how we will live our lives. Such a belief is consistent with a divine tinkerer who is learning as he goes. Such a belief is consistent with a god who created the quantum wave fluctuation that produced this universe as his last act before committing suicide. Such a belief is consistent with a creator god who guides the universe ultimately toward an evil purpose, but who has chosen to maliciously present himself as benevolent to play a trick on us. If this god existed then all of the evidence leading David to conclude a good God exists is planted there to deceive us by such a god. David rejects these other god-hypotheses, but why? I can see no reasonable objection to these other god-hypotheses. They are just as possible as his god-hypothesis. That is why scientists cannot posit theistic explanations for answers to the origin of the universe. For once we allow supernatural explanations into our equations then most any god will do, since there seems to be no way to exclude them.

A second double standard concerns science itself. Science, you know, that which brought in modernity; that which you depend on for all of your modern comforts; that which you accept in most every area of your life except when it conflicts with your Holy Book. Believers accept its results in chemistry, physics, meteorology, mechanics, forensic science, medical science, rocket science, computer science, earth science, and so forth, but they reject it when most all scientific studies tell us petitionary prayer is not efficacious, that evolutionary science shows that all present life forms have common ancestors, or that dead people do not rise from the dead.

Christians must regularly denigrate science in order to believe. They may claim their beliefs are outside of the bounds of science, or that the scientific method itself is problematical. But what better alternative is there for understanding our universe? There is none! Why should we take seriously the musings of ancient superstitious Biblical writers when it's clear they believed in a flat earth that had a solid dome above it where the sun moon and stars moved across it, and from which God send a worldwide flood? Sorry, but there is no reason why any intelligent person living in today's world should prefer the Bible over modern science. I accept all of the results of science, not just some of them.

The only kind of scientific evidence believers have on their side is something called negative evidence, which is arguing from ignorance, a known fallacy. Believers claim that since science cannot explain something therefore their particular God did it. The gaps in our understanding lead them to postulate their god from out of the many other possible gods. But that's the problem. Different religious believers around the globe can just insert their own god into the gap. There is no good way to distinguish which god best explains the gap.

There will always be scientific mysteries. The real issue that needs to be addressed is why science is closing these gaps one by one by assuming a natural explanation. If it depended on theology, we wouldn't continue seeking answers. In fact, theology stops us dead in our tracks with a "my particular God did it" explanation that squelches all scientific curiosity.

A third double standard is that Christians value faith over reason whenever they clash with each other. Who on earth would ever publicly admit this since faith can lead to many bizarre claims? What gives Christians the right to do this when they don't allow anyone else to do this same thing? They don't allow a Muslim or a Mormon this same epistemic right.

Faith is a wrongheaded psychological leap beyond what evidential reasoning leads us to accept. It fills in the gaps of the probabilities with some kind of certitude for most believers. Christians act as if they are 100% sure. You cannot be 100% sure of much of anything. Even if there is a 51% probability that Christianity is true then to conclude anything beyond that is an unjustified leap of faith, and I absolutely reject faith-based reasoning like that. It causes believers to pray rather than take their children to the doctor. It causes believers to be more trusting of other people because they trust in God. It causes believers to take completely unjustified financial risks. It causes believers to accept social injustice because of a hope for heaven. It causes believers to support abstinence-only sex education programs. It causes believers to prohibit brain stem research. It causes believers to unquestionably support Israel which in turn provokes Muslim aggression. It causes believers to sell everything and wait on a hill top for Jesus to return.

But the fact is that belief in the Christian God has no hard evidence for it. There are reasonable alternative natural explanations for every specific Christian claim. Nothing that Christians point to requires the existence of their God, whether it's religious experience, the need for morality, the evidence for life after death, or the resurrection of Jesus. There is no hard evidence to believe. Hard evidence convinces others.

Faith actually blinds believers from seeing what the actual probabilities are. Here are three examples. 1) When it comes to historical conclusions there is always the chance that contrary evidence was lost or destroyed. Historical reconstructions can never be as certain as scientific evidence or logic. 2) When it comes to biological life it's too imperfect, too filled with useless appendages that it doesn't look like what we'd expect if it were the result of intelligent design. Life looks just as it should if it's the result of the unguided process of evolution. 3) When it comes to the beginning of this universe cosmologists today agree that quantum mechanics prevented there ever being a cosmic singularity. The universe was never an infinitesimal point in space-time, and so there is no basis to assume that time began with the big bang. Stephen Hawking changed his mind on this but it has been ignored by apologists. You can read what he said on page 50 in his book *A Brief History of Time*, published in 1988.

A fourth double standard comes from global religious diversity. Is it not obvious that had David been born in a Muslim rather than Christian culture that he would be defending Allah tonight with the same passion? I wasn't born skeptical. None of us were. We were all raised as believers. We were taught to believe what our parents told us. If they said there is a Santa Claus, then he existed until they said otherwise. If we were told there was a god named Zeus we would've believed it. The problem is that our parents never told us God didn't exist because their parents never told them.

All Christians must do is to apply the same level of skepticism to their own religion as they do to the religions of others. This is what I call the *Outsider Test for Faith*. I find the Christian religion to be a delusion for the same reasons Christians find the beliefs of Mormons, Scientologists, and Jehovah's Witnesses delusional. When Christians understand why they dismiss all other religions, they will understand why I dismiss theirs. If Christians refuse to do this, then I merely ask them why the double standard? Why treat other religions differently than you do your own? I don't find any way around this test. Believers should be skeptical of what they were taught to believe given the proliferation of so many other religions and sects. After all, brainwashed people do not know they are brainwashed. The only antidote is to require hard evidence for what you believe, which is something Christians demand of the other religions they reject.

The bottom line is that when it comes to Christianity, I agree with the Protestant criticisms of the Catholics as well as the Catholic criticisms of the Protestants. And I also agree with the fundamentalist criticisms of the liberals as well as the liberal criticisms of the fundamentalists. And I agree with the Hindu, Muslim and Jewish criticisms of Christianity, as well as the Christian criticisms of their religions. When they criticize each other, I think they're all right! What's left is the demise of religion and Christianity as a whole.

A fifth double standard is how Christians assess the Bible itself. Isn't it obvious that the Bible was written from the perspective of a superstitious and pre-scientific people? Who else would believe that god-like beings could co-habit with the daughters of men, or that Jacob could increase his flock of sheep using mandrakes, or believe that the magicians in Moses' day could turn their staffs into snakes, or accept a challenge to call down fire from the sky, or cast lots during a storm to see which god sent it? Can you even imagine any judge today deciding a case by casting lots? As such I have no reason to believe the Bible. There is no way David would accept any of these claims if someone else made them. The 6th century BCE Greek historian Herodotus claimed that a horse gave birth to rabbits, that some ants were as big as foxes, and that cooked fish were resurrected from the dead. He is known as the father of history because he checked his sources. But, even with these credentials, David would never believe him about these things. So again, why the double standard? Why does he not believe Herodotus but believes Jesus and the saints all popped out of their graves?

This brings up a sixth double standard. If logic tells Christians that a belief is improbable then the evidence to the contrary must be overwhelming or else be judged faulty. Take for example miracles. Even if miracles have taken place in the past, we cannot reasonably claim that they have, for in order to do so believers must meet an almost impossible double burden of proof. For a miraculous event must be both very improbable and probable at the same time. In order to argue an event is miraculous the apologist must show that such an event is exceedingly improbable. But then the apologist must turn right around and claim this same exceedingly improbable event took place anyway.

But we're not done yet, for on top of believing these miracles took place, the doctrines derived from them cannot be logically explained, like the relationship of the three persons in the trinity, the logical coherence of incarnation of a person who is 100% God and 100% man, how the death of Jesus can possibly atone for sins, and how there can even be a resurrected body. So if given the choice between believing in the weak evidence from history, or in following the sheer logical improbability with regard to these doctrines, I must go logic every single time, just like believers do when it comes to miraculous claims they reject.

There is a seventh double standard, what I call the Problem of Miscommunication. Isn't it a no-brainer that if God exists, he has not communicated his perfect will to the Church down through the centuries? A good foreknowing God could easily have communicated better, such that there would be no Inquisition, witch hunts, heresy trials, female subjugation, Crusades, or institutional slavery. All he had to do was replace the 10th commandment about coveting, which is a thought crime, and say instead:

25

"Thou shalt not steal land in my name, treat woman as inferior, own slaves, or kill people who believe differently." And he could've communicated doctrine better too. During the eight French Wars of Religion and the Thirty Years War eight million Christians killed each other, in large part over doctrine! It was a Christian bloodbath that decimated Germany. Catholics killed Protestants and Protestants killed Catholics and each other with a religious fervor that would make Hitler jealous. If they had modern weapons of war, we can only imagine what would've happened to Europe as a whole.

By contrast, David would be the first one to blame any CEO if his company was divided like this and producing so much mayhem. With any company like this, the buck stops with the CEO. He is at least partially to blame for not communicating what he wants his company to do. Why does David hold CEOs to a higher standard than he does with his God?

This brings me to my eighth and last double standard. David holds human beings to a higher standard than he holds his God to. We are commanded to care about others, and if we don't, we have done wrong. But he exempts God from the very commands he gave to us. Why must we do as he says rather than as he does? The Bible depicts God as a barbaric tribal god who commands what every decent person today would reject.

If God existed, then, like a good parent, he would not allow us abuse the freedom he gave us. The giver of a gift is blameworthy if he gives gifts to those whom he knows will terribly abuse those gifts. Any mother who gives a razor blade to a two-year-old is culpable if that child hurts himself or others with it. Good mothers only give their children more and more freedom to do what they want so long as they are responsible with their freedom. It's that simple.

If God existed, then the 2004 Indonesian tsunami that killed a quarter of a million people should never have occurred. If God had prevented it, none of us would ever know he kept it from happening, precisely because it didn't happen. This goes for the disaster in Haiti too. Furthermore, the amount of animal suffering is atrocious as they prey on one another to feed themselves when a good God could've created us all as vegetarians in the first place. God could've created all human beings with one color of skin too. Then there would be no racism or race-based slavery. God could've created us with much stronger immune systems such that there would be no pandemics which have decimated whole populations of people. Any human being would be morally required to avert this kind of suffering based on the

Golden Rule. But David's God is exempt and yet he still wants to call God good and human beings evil.

One major Christian objection is that if God had created the universe differently it would upset the present ecosystem and/or go against the laws of nature. But as David Hume said, it seems patently obvious that the operation of the world by natural laws "seems nowise necessary for God." An omnipotent God could do perpetual miracles, and if not, why not? I call this the Perpetual Miracle Objection and I have not heard one reasonable response to it from Christian defenders of the faith. Only if Christians expect very little from an omnipotent God can they defend his ways.

So there is something seriously wrong with how Christians judge their faith. David holds other god-hypotheses to a much higher standard than his own. He accepts the results of science in every area but those few which his Holy Book claims otherwise. He values faith over reason and this blinds him to the actual probabilities. He does not evaluate his own culturally given faith with the same level of skepticism he uses to evaluate others. He accepts the claims of miracles in the Bible but denies those that come from anyone else. He accepts poor historical evidence over logical improbabilities. He holds the communication skills of a CEO to a higher standard than he does an omniscient God. And finally, David holds human beings to a higher moral standard than he holds his God to.

Christians hold to far too many double standards. For this reason, I must object to how Christians judge this case. Their thumbs are on the scales of justice. I object to their rulings. Their God does not exist.

3 – Does the Christian God Exist? Loftus vs Dinesh D'Souza

[Disclaimer: This chapter, of all the following chapters, contains the most repetition, as the debate was broadly on the same subject as the previous debate. Feel free to move to the next chapter, or stand by Zig Ziglar's maxim: "Repetition is the mother of learning, the father of action, which makes it the architect of accomplishment."]

I'm going to offer several arguments based on facts we should all agree on that show the Christian God does not exist. My claim is that these facts will force Dinesh into arguing over and over for what I'll call the Dumb and Dumber Defense, based on the movie with that title starring Jim Carrey. In every single case, Dinesh's response will be pretty much the same. Rather than admit his faith is improbable, he will be forced to claim that what he's defending is still possible despite these facts. But remember, it's possible that Jim Carrey could've gotten the girl of his dreams in the movie too. The girl said he had a "one in a million" chance at doing so.

Isn't it obvious that had Dinesh been born of Muslim rather than Christian parents he would be defending Allah tonight with the same passion? I wasn't born skeptical. None of us were. We were all raised as believers. We initially believed whatever our parents told us. If they said there is a Santa Claus, then he existed until they said otherwise. If we were told there was a god named Zeus, we would've believed it. The problem is that our parents never told us the Christian God didn't exist because their parents never told them.

So given the proliferation of so many other religions and sects around the world, we must learn to be critical of what we were raised to believe in our Christian culture. After all, brainwashed people do not know that they are brainwashed. To do this we must apply the same level of skepticism to our own inherited religion as we do to the religions of others. When Christians understand why they dismiss all other religions, they will understand why I dismiss theirs.

I think there is enough evidence to settle these religious disputes though, but only if people demand hard evidence for what they believe, like I do. Christians likewise demand hard evidence when they argue against other religions by claiming they lack it. When it comes to Christianity, I agree with the Protestant criticisms of Catholicism as well as Catholic criticisms of Protestants. And I agree with the fundamentalist criticisms of liberals as well as liberal criticisms of fundamentalists. I agree with Muslim and Jewish criticisms of Christianity, as well as Christian criticisms of other world religions. When they criticize each other, I think they're all right! What's left is the demise of Christianity and religion as a whole.

The sad fact is that believers do not dispassionately evaluate the evidence for their culturally inherited religious faith. It's crystal clear from a number of psychological studies that people are heavily influenced by non-rational factors and woefully inadequate at evidential reasoning skills; all of us, about most everything. All of us believe what we prefer to be true and we defend that which brings us Power, Money and/or Sex, what the three masters of suspicion, Nietzsche, Marx, and Freud argued. Since we can so easily be led to believe and defend what we want to be true, we must insist on having hard evidence for what we'll accept. We should demand this of the Christian God just as surely as Christians demand it of the other gods they reject. It's that simple. If God supposedly created us with minds that require evidence before we accept something, then it stands to reason he wouldn't create us this way and not also provide us what we need to believe.

In Dinesh's book, *What's So Great About Christianity*, he presents very little positive evidence for the Christian God that excludes alternative conclusions. I'm very surprised he doesn't even realize this. He argues that most people in our western culture believe, that Christianity is growing in the world, and that Christianity is unique. Of course, these claims are all at true. Tell us something we don't know next time, okay? He also claims it's beneficial to believe, although in the process Dinesh paints an unbalanced and sometimes ignorant rosy picture of Christianity, especially when it comes to the basis for morality, the origins of democracy and science. It is not true Christianity can take credit for all that's good in our society. And it is not true Christianity caused no serious harms either. Human morality and politics are human inventions which have evolved over time, just as our scientific understandings of the world. It's that simple. But this is pretty much all you'll find in his book.

Religions are human inventions too. And they too evolve. They are inextricably linked with their given cultures. So it stands to reason that any given religion is beneficial to its particular culture because as a human invention it helped to make that culture in the first place, even if they could all be greatly improved with a healthy dose of skepticism. Just ask an Amish person if his religion has social benefits, or a Buddhist in Thailand, or a Shintoist in Japan, and they will all say it does, and that their culture is better than ours, and that this shows their religion is true. And it's patently obvious that non-Christian cultures, most notably ancient Greece and Rome, have done just fine without any Christian influence at all.

So there just isn't anything in Dinesh's book that shows his particular evolving branch of Christianity is true or any of its many other different culturally produced sects. All we find in it are things that, even if shown to be true, are consistent with his faith. But just showing that something is consistent with his faith does not show his faith is probable. That's a huge non-sequitur. For instance, even if Dinesh can successfully argue that our universe began to exist and that this is consistent with his belief that there is a creator, so what? Such a belief is shared by other monotheistic religions and/or deism. Such a belief is consistent with a god who created this world as nothing more than a scientific experiment who thinks of us as rats in a maze, wondering what we will conclude about it all and how we will live our lives. Such a belief is consistent with a creator god who guides the universe ultimately toward an evil purpose, but has chosen to maliciously present himself as benevolent to play a trick on us. Such a belief is consistent with a divine tinkerer who is learning as he goes. Such a belief is also consistent with a god who created the quantum wave fluctuation that produced this universe as his last act before committing suicide. For once we allow supernatural explanations into our equations then any god will do. And this is why scientists cannot punt to theistic explanations like this.

But, in fact, cosmologists today agree that quantum mechanics prevented there ever being a cosmic singularity. The universe was never an infinitesimal point in space-time, and so there is no basis to assume that time began with the big bang. Cosmologists have published several plausible scenarios by which our universe appeared by quantum tunneling from a pre-existing universe and that time, had no beginning.

In his book, Dinesh offers nothing by way of a response to these other scenarios and he seems unaware of the work of cosmologists for the

31

last 20 years. It's as if he is oblivious to these things, because his faith has a brainwashing and blinding effect. And while he does argue miracles are possible, he offers very little to support the reliability of the Bible or evidence to show that a miracle actually occurred in the ancient biblical world.

But when it comes to the Bible isn't it obvious that it was written from the perspective of a barbaric, superstitious and pre-scientific people? Who else would believe that god-like beings could co-habit with the daughters of men, or that Jacob could increase his flock of sheep using mandrakes, or that the magicians in Moses' day could turn their staffs into snakes, or that people actually responded to a challenge to call down fire from the sky, or cast lots in a boat during a storm to see which god sent it? Can you imagine any judge today deciding a case by casting lots? And if Balaam walked into a bar and said his ass talked Dinesh would not believe it until Balaam made his ass talk. And neither would you. We also find genocide and child sacrifice commanded by the tribal god in the Bible, and the warning that an eternal punishment in hell awaits those who don't believe. There are a lot of reasons not to believe the Bible: It's inconsistent with itself, not supported by archaeology, contains fairy tales, failed prophecies, and many forgeries.

Isn't it clear that evidence from the historical past is inadequate for believing in specific doctrines that cannot be rationally explained? Historical evidence is considered so poor as evidence that all philosophers of history agree there is no such thing as objective historical writing. History is all in the mind, a few have said. At the very least it seems that almost anything can be rationally denied in the past even if it happened. And this applies even more forcefully to extraordinary claims of miracles in the past. Historians must write history from their perspective. They cannot do otherwise. They must judge the past by the standards of today, and by today's standards miracles do not happen. After all, a report of a miracle is not the same thing as experiencing one. Even if miracles have taken place, we have no reason to believe they have. Dinesh must meet an almost impossible double burden of proof here. For in order to argue an event is miraculous he must first show the event is extremely improbable given natural laws. But then he must turn right around and claim that this same extremely improbable event took place anyway.

On top of this, there is the dubious nature of the doctrines derived from these miraculous claims. They cannot be rationally explained, like the relationship of the three persons in the trinity, the logical coherence of the incarnation of a person who is 100% God and 100% man, how the death of Jesus can possibly atone for sins, and how there can be a resurrected body. So if given the choice between believing in the poor evidence of history, or in following the sheer logical improbability with regard to these doctrines, I must go with reason every single time.

And isn't it a no-brainer that if God exists, he has not communicated his perfect will to the Church down through the centuries? A good fore-knowing God could easily have communicated better, such that there would be no Inquisition, witch hunts, heresy trials, female subjugation, Crusades, or institutional slavery. All he had to do is replace the tenth commandment, which is a thought crime about coveting, with something like this: "Thou shalt not kill people with different beliefs, treat women as inferior, steal land in my name, or own slaves." And he could have communicated doctrine better too. During the eight French Wars of Religion and the Thirty Years War eight million Christians killed each other, in large part over doctrine! It was a Christian bloodbath that decimated Germany. Catholics killed Protestants, Protestants killed Catholics, and Protestants killed each other with a religious fever that would make Hitler jealous. If they had modern weapons of war, we can only imagine what would've happened to Europe as a whole. All Jesus had to do was clearly say he was establishing a church and who was to run it. All Jesus had to clearly say was whether or not the Eucharist was literally his flesh and blood. It's that simple. Out of this conflict religious tolerance was born and with it the basis for modern democracy, something we find precursors of in ancient Greece.

If God is perfectly good, all-knowing, and all-powerful, then the amount of massive suffering in this world is as close to an empirical refutation of the Christian concept of God as is possible. If God exists then like a good parent, he would not allow us to abuse the freedom he gave us. The giver of a gift is blameworthy if he gives gifts to those whom he knows will terribly abuse those gifts. Any mother who gives a razor blade to a two-year-old is culpable if that child hurts himself or others with it. Good mothers only give their children more and more freedom to do what they want so long as they are responsible with their freedom. It's that simple.

If God exists then the 2004 Indonesian tsunami that killed a quarter of a million people should never have occurred. If God had prevented it, none of us would even know he kept it from happening, precisely because it didn't happen. This goes for the disaster in Haiti too.

Furthermore, the amount of animal suffering is atrocious as they prey on one another to feed themselves when a good God could've created us all as vegetarians in the first place. God could've created all human beings with one color of skin too. Then there would be no racism or race-based slavery. God could've created us with much stronger immune systems such that there would be no pandemics which have decimated whole populations of people.

The major Christian objection is that if God had created the universe differently it would upset the present ecosystem and/or go against the laws of nature. But as David Hume said, it seems patently obvious that the operation of the world by natural laws "seems nowise necessary for God." An omnipotent God could do perpetual miracles, and if not, why not? Only if Christians expect very little from an omnipotent God can they defend his ways.

There are other things I could argue, but I'll stop here. Dinesh knows my answers to nearly all of his objections. I suspect he will offer his objections anyway, in hopes few people here have read my book.

4 – Is Religious Faith Reasonable: Loftus vs Dr. Jim Spiegel

I'm very grateful and honored to be here tonight, and I thank everyone who made this possible, especially my new friend, Professor Jim, who has agreed to try defending what cannot be reasonably defended.

Jim, I'm going to ask believers to do something, and I'd prefer it if you didn't respond just yet. Please raise your hand if you're certain or nearly certain your religious faith is correct. You have little or no doubt your faith is true. Thank you! Maybe the rest of you are probably nonbelievers. My goal is to show you have a false unreasonable misplaced sense of certainty, which is a by-product of your faith. If I can just show this, will you concede a win for me tonight? I aim to do more than that, but it's my bare minimum goal.

You realize, don't you, that you cannot all be right about your religious faith, much less certain about it? Not all of you have the same exact faith, so how can people who believe differently all be certain they are correct? Most all of you have adopted the religious faith of your parents to a great degree. Coming from a long line of Irish Catholics, I was raised to be a Catholic by my parents too. Can you be certain you were raised by the right parents who just happened to have the correct religious faith? You could have been raised to believe differently by different parents. Religious faiths are almost always products of when and where you were born, by the parents who indoctrinated you to believe. As this happened to you, it happened to your parents before you, and their parents, and their parents before them, just like it happened to my parents before me.

By definition, faith is always about that which has low probabilities. Actions based on faith are risky, are they not? Yet faith produces certainty. How is that even possible?

The fact is you cannot claim to believe what you do with certainty. Otherwise, why not say you know it, rather than that you believe it? Surely you know lots of things that have a greater degree of probability than that, most notably that you are here experiencing all the sights and sounds in this room right now. The certainty you claim is doing little more than pretending what isn't true. It's a very clear indication you need to rethink your religious faith.

Neurologist Robert Burton explains this misplaced sense of certainty this way, "Despite how certainty feels, it is neither a conscious choice nor even a thought process. The sense of certainty arises out of involuntary brain mechanisms that, like love or anger, function independently of reason." Burton says "the feeling of certainty should be thought of as one of our emotions, just like anger, pleasure, or fear. This feeling is unrelated to the strength of the evidence of what we believe. This feeling of certainty can be extremely powerful—so much so that it wins despite contrary evidence that should mitigate it. Not only this, but our brains are very good at making up reasons to justify this feeling of certainty rather than following the evidence to the reasonable conclusions."[1]

Dr. Jonas Kaplan is an assistant research professor of psychology at the University of Southern California. He and his research team studied the brain scans of people while being challenged about their political beliefs. The study uncovered a correlation: When a belief is directly challenged by new information, the brain kicks into defensive mode exactly as if it was being physically threatened. Kaplan: "The brain can be thought of as a very sophisticated self-defense machine. If there is a belief that the brain considers part of who we are, it turns on its self-defense mode to protect that belief."[2]

I am an atheist and I'm here to convince you there is no God. Did you feel that? You may have felt physical discomfort. That's your brain kicking in. How can you hope to honestly investigate this question if your brain won't let you?

Author Guy Harrison put the problem this way. When someone challenges an important belief "the brain is likely to instinctively go into siege mode. The drawbridge is raised, crocodiles are released into the moat, and defenders man the walls." He goes on to say, "The worst part of all this

[1] Burton, Robert (2009), *On Being Certain: Believing You Are Right Even When You're Not*, New York: St. Martin's Press.
[2] Jonas Kaplan, interviewed in Rydberg, Jonathan (2018), "The brain treats questions about beliefs like physical threats. Can we learn to disarm it?", *Massive Science*, https://massivesci.com/articles/brain-political-beliefs-reaction-politics/ (Accessed 05/12/2022).

is that the believer usually doesn't recognize how biased and close-minded he is. He likely feels that he is completely rational and fair."[1]

Billionaire stock investor extraordinaire, Warren Buffett tells us, "What the human being is best at doing is interpreting all new information so that their prior conclusions remain intact."

If this applies to political beliefs and investing in the stock market how much more does it apply to one's religious faith? Most people identify with their faith so much so, it defines who they are. And that kind of belief will be defended by the brain more than all others.

The job of the evolved human brain is not primarily to get at the truth. Its primary job is to protect us from harm by keeping us in a socially acceptable caring tribal grouping with whom we feel support, and can turn to for help in times of need. This means the brain makes us conform to one's own tribe. Nonconformists could be kicked out of the tribe, and that was dangerous.

So the biggest barrier to honestly desiring the truth is our tribal grouping. You want to know the truth? You may have to love the truth more than your own tribe. Most people cannot do this. Most people don't value truth enough to do this. I asked one woman whether she honestly wanted to know if her faith was false. She said she didn't, that she was happy, and that was that. She knew the implications if she concluded it was false. It would involve some adverse social repercussions she didn't want, so she chose not even to consider whether she was wrong.

In any case, we know the human brain doesn't function quite properly. And we also know the two-step solution!

The first step is to acknowledge this problem as a serious one. [For example, Alcoholics Anonymous.] The problem is the evolved brain won't allow us to seriously entertain facts that disrupt our personal, social and tribal comfort zone. So it will do everything it can to reject them.

The second step is to resolve to disarm the brain. The rational side of the brain should take over and reject what the irrational reptilian side of our brain wants. It should demand sufficient objective evidence, scientific evidence, if possible, for what will be accepted as true.

---

[1] Harrison, Guy (2013), *Think: Why You Should Question Everything*, Amherst: Prometheus Books, p. 67.

You should do this as outsiders would as much as possible, by applying the same objective standards to your own religious sect as you do to the many other religious sects you reject. You should require the same kind of evidence as you require of an ancient Chinese religion if it made a claim about a virgin giving birth to an incarnate god. Think about this. What would it require? If you're a Christian, treat your faith as if you're non-Christian, and if you're a Muslim, treat your faith as if you're a non-Muslim, and so forth. Hypothetically become a nonbeliever. See what it looks like to someone who does not believe, like an atheist. For if it doesn't convince nonbelievers, it won't convince anyone else either. When I did this, I saw that my faith was unreasonable, just as others were.

Here are some examples: Do you really believe the Bible without any objective evidence when it says the Earth existed before the Sun, Moon and stars, which were created on the fourth day? [Day one, night and day; Day Two, the firmament in the sky and the sea; Day Three, land and vegetation; Day Four, the stars, the Sun, and the Moon] Do you really have any objective evidence that a snake or a donkey talked? What about a sun standing still in the sky? Or backing up? Or turning red as blood? Or blackening out for three hours? Is there any objective evidence that a star led three astrologers to a manger in Bethlehem and hovered over it? ["The star they had seen went ahead of them until it stopped over the place where the child was." Matthew 2:1-12]. What actual evidence is there that a virgin conceived an incarnate Son of God? What about Jesus levitating with two dead men in front of the disciples, or soaring up into the sky? What about the claim that dead people arose from the grave when Jesus died, waited in their tombs for three days, then appeared in Jerusalem along with Jesus on Easter Sunday? What about the claims that shadows, clothing, pools, and handkerchiefs healed people?

Religious faith cults make these types of claims. All the time. Braco "the Gazer" is believed to heal people by simply gazing into their eyes. Do you believe these things just because they say so? Of course you don't. That's because when it comes to religious sects you were not raised to believe, you demand objective evidence. But when it comes to the religious sect you were raised to believe, you don't.

Rene Descartes is considered the father of modern philosophy. He said: "If you would be a real seeker after truth, it is necessary that at least once in your life, you doubt, as far as possible, all things." Comparatively speaking, believers just don't do this. Hardly ever! It should be a rite of passage into adulthood. When challenged, like I'm doing now, their brains will convince them that reading books by authors who defend their own religious sect is doing all that's required. But doing so is seeking to confirm what they already believe. If you aren't reading books outside your comfort zone you're not really searching for the truth. You are scared of the truth. This is your brain in action.

Don't pat yourselves on the back too much for being here tonight. That doesn't mean you're interested in the truth. My guess is you're here to root Jim on, hoping he demolishes me.

So, is religious faith reasonable?

No! The answer can even be found in the definitions of the terms used.

To be "religious" is to accept the claim that there is a superhuman deity, most notably a personal creator god, who is to be worshipped and obeyed.

To be "reasonable" is to follow the rules of logic, and to require sufficient objective evidence for knowledge claims about the world we live in, including the religious claim that a personal creator god exists.

To have "faith" is to accept a claim based on flawed reasoning and insufficient objective evidence. For our purposes, it's to accept a miraculous claim as true, such as a virgin giving birth to an incarnate son of God, without sufficient objective verifiable evidence. It's to allow the reptilian brain to keep us away from honesty seeking the truth by a number of cognitive biases, most notably confirmation bias which seeks above all to confirm what one already believes, rather than to disconfirm it.

Saint Anselm's motto is the prime example of why faith is folly: "Faith seeks understanding." First, there is faith. Then believers seek to understand it by making the necessary distinctions that make it palatable, and by coming up with arguments and desperately searching for any evidence showing it's true. This is the core of what confirmation bias is all about! By following Anselm's motto Christian defenders can and do avoid any and all evidence to the contrary if they can get away with it. Philosopher Stephen Law explains: "Anything based on faith, no matter how ludicrous, can be made to be consistent with the available evidence, given a little patience and ingenuity."[1] They've had about 2000 years to do this. Anthropologist James Houk illustrates that "virtually anything and everything, no matter how absurd, inane, or ridiculous, has been believed or claimed to be true at one time or another by somebody, somewhere in the name of faith."[2]

Therefore, putting the definitions together, to have "religious faith" is to accept the religious claim that there is a superhuman deity, most notably a personal creator god, who is to be worshipped and obeyed, based on flawed reasoning and insufficient objective evidence.

This is not just a semantic issue. It's at the heart of our differences. BTW: Jim is wrong! If faith is trust there is no reason to trust faith. If we are to trust in God, we need to have sufficient evidence to know that he exists and that he can be trusted.

The only sense I can make of the way believers use the word "faith" is that it's an irrational leap over the probabilities. They add faith to the low probabilities in order to stretch an "improbable" conclusion to reach a "probable" one, and that is quite simply irrational.

I'm arguing along with atheist author George Smith that "faith as an alleged method of acquiring knowledge, is totally invalid."[3] It's not just your religious dogmas that are unreasonable. It's how you arrive at and maintain them. For as Peter Boghossian has argued, "Belief in God is not the problem. Belief without evidence is the problem. Warrantless, dogged confidence is the problem." He adds, "The most charitable thing we can say about faith is that it's likely to be false."[4]

When we have sound reasoning based on sufficient objective evidence faith adds nothing to our conclusions. Faith has no method for acquiring objective knowledge. Faith is folly. Reasonable people should all think exclusively in terms of the probabilities by "proportioning their conclusions according to the strength of the evidence", as philosopher par excellence David Hume said. When you do that, you'll see why religious faith is unreasonable.

---

[1] Law, Stephen (2011), *Believing Bullshit*, Amherst: Prometheus Books, p. 75.
[2] Houk, James T. (2017), *The Illusion of Certainty,* Amherst: Prometheus Books p. 16.
[3] Smith, George (1989), *Atheism: The Case Against God*, Amherst: Prometheus Books, p. 120.
[4] Boghossian, Peter (2013), *A Manual for Creating Atheists*, Durham, NC: Pitchstone Publishing, p. 77.

These following pages contain extras I used as supplementary material in subsequent rebuttals:

Christianity is Unworthy of Thinking Adults: Three Decisive Cases in Point

1) Case in Point One: Even Christians Agree Faith is Opposed to Reason

According to Paul in Colossians 2:8, "See no one takes you captive through hollow and deceptive philosophy." Jesus purportedly said, "I praise you, Father, Lord of heaven and earth, because you have hidden these things from the wise and learned, and revealed them to little children. Yes, Father, for this was your good pleasure." (Luke 10:21). Paul wrote, "The message of the cross is foolishness to those who are perishing, but to us who are being saved it is the power of God. For it is written: 'I will destroy the wisdom of the wise; the intelligence of the intelligent I will frustrate.' Where is the wise man? Where is the scholar? Where is the philosopher of this age? Has not God made foolish the wisdom of the world?... For the foolishness of God is wiser than man's wisdom" (1 Cor. 1:18–25). Tertullian (160–220 CE) asked: "What has Athens to do with Jerusalem?" In words reminiscent of Søren Kierkegaard, Tertullian wrote of the incarnation of Jesus by saying, "Just because it is absurd, it is to be believed . . . it is certain because it is impossible." Martin Luther called reason "the Devil's Whore." As such, reason "can do nothing but slander and harm all that God says and does." Immanuel Kant said that he "found it necessary to deny knowledge of God...in order to find a place for faith." William Lane Craig agrees with Luther's viewpoint. He argues that "reason is a tool to help us better understand our faith. Should faith and reason conflict, it is reason that must submit to faith, not vice versa."

There is something wrong with a religious faith that needs to disparage reason like this. It's admitting Christianity cannot be defended by reason. If that's what they think, why should we think otherwise? Why should anyone? I see no reason to do so.

2) Case in Point Two: Why Should We Believe If the Jews Didn't?

41

The most plausible estimate of the first-century Jewish population comes from a census of the Roman Empire during the reign of Claudius (48 CE) that counted nearly 7 million Jews. If we add in the Jews outside the Roman Empire in places like Babylon, the total first-century Jewish population could have been 8 million. It's estimated that there may have been as many as 2.5 million Jews in Palestine.

These Jews believed in God. They were beloved by their God. They believed their God did miracles. They hoped for a Messiah. They knew well their Old Testament prophecies. Yet the overwhelming majority of them did not believe Jesus was raised from the dead. Catholic New Testament scholar David C. Sim argued: "Throughout the first century the total number of Jews in the Christian movement probably never exceeded 1,000 and by the end of the century the Christian church was largely Gentile."[1]

Since Jews were there and they didn't believe, why should we? Why should anyone? I see no reason to do so.

The Christian response is that these Jews didn't want to believe because Jesus was not their kind of Messiah, a king who would throw off Roman rule. But then, where did they get that idea in the first place? They got it from their own Scriptures. And who supposedly inspired them? Their God. This means that even though their God loved them over all others, s/he purposely misled them, thereby condemned them to hell along with centuries of persecution as "Christ-killers" for following reason. For there is no prophecy in the Old Testament to be regarded as a prophecy that points exclusively to Jesus as the Messiah. The Psalmist literature therefore doesn't count! Sure, there are passages that describe a hope for a political Messiah, but that doesn't make them predictions. All a reasonable person needs to do is look in the New Testament for the claims of fulfilled prophecy. Follow them back to the source in the Old Testament, then study the context. The young girl who was to give birth in Isaiah 7 was not a virgin, and it clearly is not speaking of the distant future. The suffering servant passage in Isaiah 53 is speaking of the sufferings of Israel as a nation, not the Messiah (Isaiah 49:3). There is no hint in the OT texts that any "double-

---

[1] Sim, David C. (2005), "How many Jews became Christians in the first century? The failure of the Christian mission to the Jews," *Theological Studies*, 61, No 1/2, https://hts.org.za/index.php/HTS/article/view/430, (Accessed 04/20/2022).

fulfilment" is possible. Stretching these and other so-called OT prophecies to Jesus is mishandling the texts based on faith.

3) Case In Point Three: Not Even Christian Apologists Believe Sufficient Evidence Exists.

Most of the best Christian defenders admit there isn't sufficient objective evidence to believe, perhaps upwards to 80% of them. Alvin Plantinga has even argued Christian believers do not need objective evidence for their faith.

They argue the evidence alone won't convince people so they must first effectively show that God exists. They reason like this: "Only if people are brought to first believe in a miracle-working god can the available evidence convince them Jesus was raised from the dead."

Still, others came along and were forced to admit there aren't even any good arguments for the existence of God. Alvin Plantinga: "I don't know of an argument for Christian belief that seems very likely to convince one who doesn't already accept its conclusion." [*Warranted Christian Belief*, p. 201.] John Feinberg: "I wouldn't try to prove God's existence first, if at all, in that I am not convinced that any of the traditional arguments succeeds." [*Can You Believe It's True: Christian Apologetics in a Modern, Postmodern Era*, p. 321]. Richard Swinburne: "I cannot see any force in an argument to the existence of God from the existence of morality." [*The Existence of God* 2nd, ed., p. 215.][1]

Now what? Did they abandon their attempts to defend Christianity? NO! Christian defenders started presupposing God exists (or even Christianity as a whole), without objective evidence or arguments to the existence of God. Thus begging the whole question.

Still, other Christian defenders argued against the attempt to rationally defend their faith. They insist God must be personally experienced instead. This abandons the rational attempt to show the Christian faith is true. Subjective experiences don't say anything objective about the objective world.

---

[1] Loftus, John W. (2018),"Three Top Apologists Reject the Force Of Arguments To God's Existence," *Debunking Christianity*, https://www.debunking-christianity.com/2018/12/three-top-apologists-reject-force-of.html, (Accessed 04/20/2022).

Finally, many of them now embrace an eclectic or pragmatic means of defending their faith, where the conclusion largely dictates the means. Christianity is the conclusion. Now use whatever means is needed to reach that conclusion.

Christian believers who say their faith is based upon sufficient objective evidence just don't understand what's been going on behind the scenes in the hallways of their seminaries. Even most of the best Christian defenders/apologists acknowledge the evidence just isn't there. Instead of acknowledging this fact, they concocted several other bogus ways to defend their faith, ones they would never accept if these same rationalizations came from any other religious sect. Since there are five means to defend Christianity (above) and only one of them advocates objective evidence exists to believe, four of them--or 80% of them--reject evidence as primary. Just consider what would've been the case if sufficient objective evidence existed. Then no other means to defend the Christian faith would've been proposed, much less adopted by many others.

If Christian defenders don't think sufficient objective evidence exists, then why should we? Why should anyone? I see no reason to do so.

This third case in point is something I argued in chapter five of my book, *How to Defend the Christian Faith: Advice from an Atheist* (which I last revised for my book, *The Case against Miracles*). I consider it the best chapter I've written in all my books. It documents what I say above. The book as a whole is recommended by a few important scholars, most notably by Christian apologist Dr. Chad Meister. He says, "In this book John Loftus provides some insightful criticisms of arguments by Christian thinkers, including those having to do with the problem of evil." You would think there was nothing he hadn't considered before, yet he says I provide "some insightful criticisms" in it. See for yourselves.

5 – Why I Am an Atheist: Loftus vs Randal Rauser

Here is my 20-minute statement on "Why I Am an Atheist" when debating Randal Rauser, co-author with me for the book, *God or Godless. One Atheist. One Christian. Twenty Controversial Questions*. It took me over forty years to write it since it's based on all that I've learned in that time.

I'm very grateful and honored to have been brought here to discuss/debate these issues. Thank you so much. This is refreshing, an indicator that you want to seriously examine your faith. I think Randal is one of the best Christian apologists of our generation. He's brilliant of course, but that's what it takes to defend the indefensible. He doesn't think atheists are necessarily crazy, and that's a plus too! He's willing to reasonably engage us and to revise his theology, if needed, in response to our arguments. So I am very grateful he chose to co-write God or Godless with me. I look forward to him revising his theology in light of tonight.

I'm going to give reasons why I am an atheist. First, what is an atheist? A-theist. Non-theist. Non-believer. I do not believe.

As a former Christian, I examined several major religions and various Christian cults and concluded there wasn't sufficient objective evidence for any of them. I was a skeptic of all other religions except my own particular evangelical sect. What happened that changed my mind is that over the years I learned to apply the same objective evidential standards to my own faith that I had already applied to the other faiths I rejected. As I did that, I learned to reject them all because of the same reason, the lack of sufficient objective evidence. [You can see this line of reasoning developed in my book, *The Outsider Test for Faith*].

Muslims respond that I willfully refuse to believe in Allah, just as Christians say I willfully refuse to believe in Yahweh. But I am no more refusing to believe in those gods and their religions as I refuse to believe in the Mormon, or Hindu gods and their religions. I just think none of them have sufficient objective evidence for them to believe. That's all there is to it.

On the topic of this talk, I wrote a 500-page book, *Why I Became an Atheist*. It's my magnum opus. If you want to read a detailed answer to this question, get that book.

One of the reasons I am an atheist is because I honestly wanted to know the truth. Most Christians do not honestly examine their faith. The overwhelming majority of them will never read that book or one like it. So if nothing else, read *God or Godless*.

Unfortunately, when we look at Randal's defense of his faith in *God or Godless*, it is entirely worthless. [Sorry to be so adversarial, but please consider I edited a book titled, *The Christian Delusion*. I do hope his arguments push other evangelicals in his direction since he is closer to the truth.] I am an atheist because even the best and brightest apologists like Randal who take our arguments seriously cannot provide a good reason to believe.

So let's revisit Randal's ten chosen topics:

1) **If there is no God then life has no meaning**. Wrong. No one should ever reject the evidence for a conclusion simply because they dislike the conclusion. If there is no God then we are our own meaning makers. Period. Only after you realize God doesn't exist will you see this.

2) **If there is no God then everything is permitted**. Wrong again. The ones doing the permitting are people in their respective societies. Even if Thomas Hobbes is correct that we are at war with everyone else, we must still adopt some kind of reasonable social contract whereby we join together for the common good. If not, a society will collapse into chaos. Since no one desires chaos there are reasonable limits to what any society will permit. By contrast, if God exists there are no limits to what can be permitted when people believe something to be divinely authorized.

3) **Science is no substitute for religion**. Bogus. If there is one mark of the deluded mind (defined as "believing against the overwhelming evidence") it's that somewhere along the line he or she must be ignorant of, or denigrate, or deny science. Religion has given us nothing in comparison to science. Faith-based reasoning processes are notoriously unreliable. They do not help us get at the truth. What do they offer as a substitute for evidence-based reasoning processes?

46

4) **God is the best explanation of the whole shebang**. Spurious. Believers have always said this, even though science has made great strides in answering this question. God of the gaps arguments like this one have failed so many times in the past it's quite surprising to see Randal still using it. Something exists. So either something—anything—has always existed, or something—anything—popped into existence out of nothing. Those are the choices. The best explanation for our existence is the simplest one. The theistic hypothesis is that a three-in-one God exists who never had a beginning or a prior moment to choose his own nature, who never learned any new propositions, who cannot think because thinking requires weighing alternatives, who cannot even laugh because nothing takes him by surprise, who created this world with its natural disasters, who doesn't even benevolently act in the midst of our sufferings. This is no explanation at all. So many questions abound. The scientific hypothesis merely starts with an equilibrium of positive and negative energy along with the laws of physics. Grant this and there is a 60% chance something should exist. Given the fact of evolution, there is no need for a God, and there's no evidence he is involved in this process at all. The main thing scientists have not yet explained is the origin of life. If your theology hangs on that gap then you are betting against everything science has solved so far. And once you allow god explanations into your equations then most any god will do, even an evil one.

5) **If there is no God then we don't know anything**. False. If so, chimps don't know anything either. They don't know how to get food, or mate or even where to live. Without knowing anything they should've died off a long time ago. And yet here they are. They don't need a god to know these things. Why do we need a god for knowledge? We learn through a process of trial and error. Since we've survived as a human species, we have acquired reliable knowledge about our world. Period.

6) **Love exists only if God exists**. Erroneous. This is an empty rhetorical claim devoid of any content at all. Believers have always said this even during the Inquisition and witch-hunts. Randal should look at the evidence of the history of the church. He should consider the other primates who exhibit characteristics of love. He should also take seriously the evidence in the Bible that God is not love either, for he will squash you like a

47

bug if you don't obey him, which isn't descriptive of love, much less parental love, or perfect love at all. It's descriptive of a despotic king, of which Yahweh was modeled after.

7) **Everybody has faith**. Misguided. This may be true for most people, but it's the problem, not the solution. Faith is a cognitive bias causing people to overestimate any confirming evidence and to underestimate any disconfirming evidence. Faith is an irrational leap over the probabilities. [When I say this I'm not saying Randal is irrational, only that faith is irrational.] Reasonable people think exclusively in terms of probabilities based on objective sufficient evidence along with sound reasoning about the evidence.

8) **Objective beauty exists; therefore, God exists**. Foolish. There is nothing objectively beautiful or ugly in the world. There is just raw uninterpreted stuff. If we could see and hear the whole electromagnetic and sonic spectra then all we could see or hear would be white noise. How is white noise objectively beautiful? Without any objective beauty, there is no argument to the existence of his evangelical God.

9) **God best explains the miracles in people's lives**. Silly. Given the number of believers in the world and the number of rare coincidences that could occur in their lives, I'm actually surprised there aren't more miracle claims. Extremely rare coincidences happen. It's what we would expect given the odds. There are no verifiable supernatural agents behind them. People merely see supernatural agents where there aren't any because we've inherited this propensity from the animal kingdom, who thought they heard predators approaching merely at the random sound of rustling leaves. What we need are clinical studies, which are the best kind of scientific evidence for these claims, and nearly every scientific study done on petitionary prayer has shown it works statistically no better than chance.

10) **God raised Jesus from the dead**. Not true. No reasonable person today should believe 2nd 3rd 4th handed testimony coming from a lone part of the ancient world as we find in 4th-century manuscripts written by pre-scientific superstitious people who doctored up and forged many of these texts. Almost all of our questions go unanswered, the kind of

questions we have been able to ask of the rise of Mormonism in the modern world, leading us to reject it. What did the early disciples actually claim to have seen? Did they all tell the same stories? Did any of them recant? All we have is Paul's first-person testimony, and if we're to believe Acts 26:19, he said his Damascus-road conversion was based on nothing more than a vision.

If we read in a 2000-year-old ancient Chinese document that a virgin had a baby, then that so-called testimonial evidence is too far removed for us to accept it. It doesn't matter if the same document tells us others at that time believed in a virgin birth. The evidence is still the same for us, since it comes from that very same document. It also doesn't matter if it was believed within a religious context. If anything, the religious context would help to discredit it, since miracle claims within religious contexts are a dime a dozen.

Apologists like Randal throw up nothing but smoke-screens to deny the obvious. They will concoct disanalogous hypothetical stories that have no bearing on the need for sufficient objective evidence. No reasonable person should believe that a virgin gave birth to God incarnate in today's world without sufficient objective evidence. Can you even imagine what evidence would convince you that she did? So why should this requirement be different when it comes to the ancient pre-scientific superstitious past? If anything, it should be foremost in our minds. Whether a virgin gave birth to God incarnate is a historical claim about what supposedly happened in the past. There is only one kind of evidence that can show this, if it can be shown at all. Objective evidence. We need a sufficient amount of it to convince us. No amount of intellectual gerrymandering can weasel out of this reasonable requirement.

Alvin Plantinga has even made a sustained case that he is rational to believe without any evidence at all, in his 500-page book Warranted Christian Belief. But it's of no use. Plantinga's argument is based on a conditional, "If...then." "If Christian belief is true, it very likely does have warrant." Well then, if Mormonism is true then it very likely does have warrant. If Scientology is true then it very likely does have warrant. If Islam is true then it very likely does have warrant. If Hinduism is true then it very likely does have warrant. This is nothing but sophisticated empty rhetoric irrelevant to the real issue of whether these religions are true. It

49

reminds me of what philosophy Professor Stephen Law wrote: "Anything based on faith, no matter how ludicrous, can be made to be consistent with the available evidence, given a little patience and ingenuity." (*Believing Bullshit*, p. 75).

Plantinga argues that beliefs based on private subjective experiences are warranted unless there is a defeater to them. The defeater to any private subjective experience is, was, and always will be, sufficient objective evidence. Objective evidence is public evidence, scientific evidence, historical evidence, evidence that convinces reasonable people. Anyone who thinks private subjective experiences count as evidence for the claims of history is not thinking rationally. In other contexts, psychics do that. Is Plantinga a psychic? Is that what he considers evidence? This is not how historians do their work, and the tools they use are all we have to know what happened in the past. A trained historian will never conclude that a miracle can be detected with those tools, for it is always more likely than not to be explained as a myth, legend, extremely rare coincidence, or lie, rather than a suspension of the laws of nature. These tales litter the ancient highway. God may even have done a plethora or miracles in the past and will do so again in the future. But the historian's perspective, the only one available, comes from the modern world where they do not happen.

Believers who claim they have had a personal experience with their particular cultural god are a dime a dozen. It doesn't matter if believers say their religious experience is real and the others are not. You would expect them to say that. The honest truth for honest people is that these subjective experiences provide no evidence at all. The very fact that believers like Plantinga deny the need for sufficient objective evidence is because they intuitively know their faith does not have it, for if it did, they would be the first ones crowing about it. If nothing else, this should serve as a red-light warning that one's faith is a delusion.

Natural theology doesn't fare any better. When it comes to Jesus there was a large group of believers who were prone to accept the tales told about him by early Christians. The Jews. They lived in the same time period, believed in Yahweh, that he does miracles, and they knew their OT prophecies. If there was ever a testing ground for the claims about Jesus, the Jews in his day were it. Yet they didn't believe. They were there and they were believers and yet the overwhelming number of them did not believe. Why should we? Who inspired these supposed OT prophecies?

Yahweh. So let me ask, were the Jews stupid or did God mislead them? Are Christians really willing to say nearly 8 million Jews at the time of Jesus were stupid? Are Christians really willing to say they did not desire to know the truth, that they insincerely preferred to believe a lie, almost all of them, such that Paul had to preach the gospel to Gentiles for converts? And if God misled them to believe a lie, then he also condemned them to hell. Which is it? The fact is there is no prophecy in the OT that is to be regarded as a prophecy that specifically points to the birth, life, death or resurrection of Jesus. None. All you need to do is read the so-called prophecies in their original contexts and you'll see that the NT writers grossly mishandled them.

Natural theology, therefore, died a long time ago, before it was born, with the Jewish rejection of Jesus as the resurrected Messiah. If there was sufficient evidence to conclude Jesus was the resurrected Messiah then almost all Jews in the first century would have become Christians. In fact, almost all theists should be Christians since they share the same belief in a creator miracle-working God. The problem is that just because someone is a theist does not mean it's more likely than not that a particular Christian miracle took place. All theism grants you is the possibility of miracles. But I too allow for them. Theists in other religions require sufficient objective evidence before accepting the miracle claims of other theistic religions. The raw uninterpreted historical data must therefore provide the reasonable theist with sufficient evidence that a God did this or that particular miracle before accepting it. So to be consistent without using any double standards, theists within their own religions should require sufficient objective evidence before believing that a theistic God did the miracles within their own religion. They must require this without begging the question or special pleading their own case.

I simply require sufficient objective evidence for them all. Remember, we're trying to find out what's true. Not what makes us feel good, but what actually accords with reality. Our feelings are only a reliable guide to subjective things, like what kind of music we enjoy, or what type of food we like, and so on. They cannot guide us to the truth about historical events. My position is the most consistent one to adopt, and given that different theists reject each other's foundational miracle claims, they do the work for me. They don't believe, just as I don't believe in any of them.

I developed some questions for Rauser beforehand:

1) If you wanted to know what happened at Custer's Last Stand wouldn't you want sufficient evidence before coming to a conclusion? Why is that different when it comes to the claim that a virgin gave birth to God incarnate?

2) Can you provide any objective evidence for your faith without special pleading or begging the question?

3) Do you reject personal private subjective experience when it comes to other religions? If so, why don't you reject those same kinds of claims when it comes to your religion?

4) Can you provide any reason at all to think that sufficient objective evidence is not good enough when it comes to any historical claim?

5) When it comes to Mohammed flying on a winged horse to visit the heavenly realms, or the golden plates that Joseph Smith supposedly translated into the Book of Mormon, or Scientologist's claim that an intergalactic emperor named Xenu placed people in a volcano and blew them up, do you require sufficient evidence in order to believe them? Why are your superstitious claims exempt from this same requirement?

6) What is the specific doctrinal content to your subjective experience of God? Does your experience provide any? What is it? If not, how can you claim your experience leads you to believe as you do? If so, what is it and why do other evangelicals who claim this same experience believe differently based on it? Do evangelical witch-hunters in Africa have the same properly basic belief about God? Specifically, with regard to salvation. Specifically, with regard to the Bible.

7) Can you explain why your so-called properly basic beliefs change with more study? Why does a child have properly basic beliefs about God that an educated Christian adult would deny?

8) Do you believe in psychics? Are you a psychic? Can you know whether

or not a virgin had a baby (or any of a number of other purported historical claims in the Bible) based on psychic abilities? Isn't claiming to know you can irrational?

9) Can you read God's mind? Every believer on the planet claims to know God's mind.

10) How do you escape the charge that you're just making stuff up as you go?

6 – Christianity or Atheism? Loftus vs Wallace Marshall

I am very honored to be here and grateful that anyone showed up at all!

My contention is that non-belief makes more sense than Marshall's Evangelical Protestant Christianity, the kind located in the western world and in the Northern hemisphere, which began with the rise of Fundamentalism in 1910. Non-belief makes more sense given the lack of scientific and historical evidence for the number of extraordinary miracle claims Marshall must defend, any one of which, if not shown correct, would sink his ship of faith.

As a former Christian apologist myself, I don't think there is sufficient evidence to believe in Christianity, or in any other religion. This is the main reason I am a non-believer, an atheist. I've discovered that no religion can be shown to be true any more than the others that exist. They all share the same grounding. They all stand on the quicksand of faith-based reasoning as opposed to science-based reasoning.

Even if I cannot explain why the universe has the complexity to allow for life on earth, or how it all originated, I know enough to reject faith-based answers. I'm going to wait on the results of science to tell me the facts of the universe. It has a really good track record. Darwin solved the origin of species question with the science of evolution. It's a problem no one could have predicted would ever be solved. So my bet is on science to solve others, if they can be solved at all. And as science answers questions religions die. For with the fact of evolution Christianity died. There is no longer an original Adam and Eve, no longer an original sin, and no need for a savior. So there's probably no creator either.

I'm thinking like a scientist, which means following David Hume's principle that a wise person proportions one's belief to the available evidence. Going beyond that is unreasonable. So I refuse to play the pretend game of faith by pretending to know more than what I can reasonably know.

Let's put this into perspective. Since non-Christians in the world number roughly 4.8 billion, I stand with the majority of people who reject

Christianity. I symbolize the position of everyone else, the billions of non-Christians in the world. It's Christianity vs. everyone else. My view is that everyone else is right!

When it comes to Marshall's type of Christianity, not many people in the world believe it. There are an estimated 285 million Evangelicals, comprising merely 13% of the total Christian population, but just 4% of the total world population. That's not too good at all, yet that's the good news. The bad news is that it's getting worse by the day. John Dickerson, in his book, *The Great Evangelical Recession*, tells us more than a quarter-million evangelical young people "walk away from Christianity each year. Of that number... 65% do not find their way back" because "they don't believe anymore."[1] We're told, "This is a trend. And the trend is one of decline."[2]

Now let's consider why the Mormon Church exists. All it took was a deceiver, or madman named Joseph Smith, and people willing to believe him. Persecution, propaganda, and high procreation rates by his polygamous followers did the rest. That's it. When it comes to one of its main claims, that Native Americans are descendants of the Israelites who supposedly came across the Atlantic around 600 BCE, DNA evidence from more than 150 Native American tribes revealed no Israelite DNA. The irrefutable conclusion is that the Book of Mormon story is fiction.

Let's next consider Scientology, which was founded by science fiction writer L. Ron Hubbard. He told us years before starting his religion, that "Writing for a penny a word is ridiculous. If a man really wants to make a million dollars, the best way would be to start his own religion." And he did. All it took was a deceiver, or madman and people willing to believe him.

These are two of the fastest-growing religions in the world, and yet they are based on lies. We know this!

We know enough about these two religions to reject them because they originated in the modern world among scientifically minded people. They also left paper trails which helped us document their lies. When it comes to Christianity, we lack the same means to evaluate its earliest origins in the first century. All we basically have is the propaganda written by Christians themselves. They excluded any contemporary writings of the

---

[1] Dickerson, John (2013), *The Great Evangelical Recession*, Ada, MI: Baker Books, pp. 98-102.
[2] Ed Stetzer as quoted in Dickerson, p. 32.

Judaizers and the Gnostics of their time. And there are no early records of its rise by the Romans or the Jews of that day.

So let me ask, how many of you, if raised to believe as Mormons or Scientologists, would ever come to the conclusion that your faith is false by reading exclusively their approved writings? Given the number of people here tonight, no one would. Likewise, how many of you, if raised to believe as Christians, would ever come to the conclusion that your faith is false by reading exclusively Christian writings? Again, probably no one. Yet that's exactly what we have in the doctored up canonized New Testament, the approved writings of Christians who won the theological wars of the ancient past. In the Gospels, for instance, Jesus always had the last word over his opponents—which is something I have never seen in any real religious debate. We never hear what his opponents said in response to him, who were surely intelligent people.

So how do you know you don't believe something that's false, or even a lie? Most people are simply born into a religion, or unreasonably persuaded to believe because of personal anecdotal evidence, or a warming of the bosom, or even peer-pressure.

This is why I've proposed and defended *The Outsider Test for Faith*, to help believers honestly evaluate their inherited faith. You must evaluate your own faith as outsiders. You must use the same reasonable standards when considering your own faith as you do when considering all other religions. No double standards. Demand the same amount of evidence for your own faith as you do for other religions. Do not try to explain away any difficulties. Deal with them honestly as you would to the other faiths you reject. Take a serious look at your faith as if you were an outsider. Use the Golden rule: Do unto your own faith what you do unto the faiths of others.

You must do this because cognitive biases get in the way of evaluating your own religious faith. The mother of all cognitive biases is confirmation bias, which is the strong tendency to search for data and/or interpret existing data in ways that confirm one's prior beliefs. This bias forces believers to misjudge the probabilities in favor of their faith. But only by looking honestly at all faiths as an outsider will help you know which religion is true, if there is one.

The reason you don't do this is because your brain will not allow you to seriously consider you might be wrong. In fact, right now your brain is ignoring the impact of what I just said. It's convincing you that what I'm saying doesn't apply to you. It's thrusting what I said back at me. Can you hear your brain say: "Loftus is the one who shouldn't trust his brain. He's the one deceived"? But I already admit this is what my brain does, so to correct for it I've learned to demand hard cold evidence before I'll accept these types of claims as true.

Here are the facts. Your brain will deceive you if left unchecked. You must force it to heel against its preferences. Your brain needs help to get at the truth. It needs better inputs, the objective inputs of science. For the brain is a belief engine. We first believe, usually what we prefer to be true, or what's familiar, then we seek to confirm our beliefs, not to disconfirm them. We grope around for evidence to support our beliefs, sometimes despite solid evidence to the contrary. Once the brain latches onto an idea it can be extremely difficult to dislodge that idea from its grasp. The more important the idea is to the brain then the less likely it can be dislodged. If left to itself your brain will try to fit all facts into a grid of self-preservation, a procrustean bed of its own making.

The brain only cares if what it concludes helps it to survive. The brain evolved to act this way for self-preservation purposes. It maintains and defends its beliefs so you can survive as a social creature, since you need others to survive! You will defend the beliefs of your social group in order to stay within the safety net of your social group, irrespective of whether those beliefs are true or not. There is a massive amount of solid research supportive of these undeniable facts.

So, again, I ask, how do you know you don't believe something that is false, or even a lie? You don't, not until you liberate your brain of confirmation bias by treating your own inherited faith just like you do with the religions you reject.

Now for some specific arguments. There are roughly five strategies (or methods) used by Christian apologists to defend the Christian faith. Let's let each one of them represent about 20% of the total apologetic strategies used by them. The first one is called *evidentialism*, where it's claimed there is sufficient objective evidence to believe. Now I disagree that there is sufficient evidence to believe, but I do agree that this is the only reasonable strategy to adopt when defending Christianity. If you disagree, just ask what you would think as outsiders, if Mormons, Scientologists, Muslim or Orthodox Jews admitted there wasn't sufficient objective evidence for their faiths. You would recognize something is seriously wrong from the start.

58

Well, something is seriously wrong with Christianity from the start. For most Christian apologists reject evidentialism. They reject the need for, and/or the existence of, sufficient objective evidence in defense of the Christian faith. That's probably because the first modern evidentialists were deists, and look where that got them. But that's where the evidence leads, away from Christianity and toward total non-belief itself. The other four major strategies are as follows:

2) **The Classical Strategy**, which I call ***Apologetics Based On Special Pleading***—getting to a god does not get you to your theistic religion;

3) **The Presuppositionalist Strategy**, which I call ***Apologetics Based On Assuming What Needs to Be Proved***—which is a known fallacy. [You just can't do that!];

4) **The Fideist Strategy**, what I call ***Apologetics Based On Private Subjective Experiences***—which are only evidence of private states of the mind; and

5) **The Cumulative Case Strategy**, what I call ***Eclectic Pragmatic Apologetics Based On Prior Conclusions***—which is a method of saying whatever works.

Further details need not concern you here. They can be found in a chapter of my book, *How to Defend the Christian Faith: Advice from an Atheist*. What should concern you is that these four different strategies all deny evidentialism, the need for, and/or the existence of, sufficient objective evidence in defense of Christianity. If these five strategies all had an equal number of Christian defenders arguing for them, that means 80% of Christian defenders reject the need for, and/or the existence of, sufficient objective evidence in defense of the Christian faith.

Be honest. If there was sufficient evidence for Christianity then no other apologetic strategy would ever have been devised! So the very fact these four other strategies exist means Christians themselves admit their faith does not have sufficient evidence for it. It's not just me saying this. It's what 80% of Christian apologists themselves admit.

What about arguments to the existence of God? Two of the greatest living Christian apologists are Alvin Plantinga and Richard Swinburne. Plantinga has admitted theistic arguments don't work, saying, "I don't know of an argument for Christian belief that seems very likely to convince one who doesn't already accept its conclusion." Swinburne specifically rejects the Moral Argument to God's existence, saying, "I cannot see any force in an argument to the existence of God from the existence of morality." Another Christian apologist of note is John Feinberg. He is on record as saying, "I am not convinced that any of the traditional arguments [for God's existence] succeeds." Now if they don't think these arguments work then why should any of us? Again, it's not just me who is saying this. It's what Christian apologists themselves say.

When it comes to the explanation of existence, we are faced with two options, that, 1) something—anything—has always existed, or 2) something—anything—popped into existence out of nothing. Either choice seems extremely unlikely. There is little in our experience that can help us choose. But one of them is correct and the other is false. We either start with the brute fact that something has always existed, or the brute fact that something popped into existence out of nothing. So the simpler our brute fact is then the more probable it is, per Ockham's razor. All that scientists have to assume is an equilibrium of positive and negative energy and the laws of physics. This is as close to nothing as science can get. But grant it and the late physicist Victor Stenger argued: "the probability for there being something rather than nothing can actually be calculated; it is over 60 percent." As such, "only by the constant action of an agent outside the universe, such as God, could a state of nothingness be maintained. The fact that we have something is just what we would expect if there is no God."

Recently two physicists have significantly revised the standard model of the Big Bang, which is based on Einstein's theory of general relativity. When they applied some quantum corrections to the model, they concluded the universe had no beginning, writing, "It existed forever as a kind of quantum potential before collapsing into the hot dense state we call the Big Bang." [This new model is being advanced by Ahmed Farag Ali at Benha University and Saurya Das at the University of Lethbridge].

By contrast, I find it implausible to believe that a Triune God has always existed and will forever exist as a fully formed being who is present everywhere. How could he have freely chosen who he is and what his values are? How is it possible that this being never had any disagreements within the godhead? How can he think, or make choices or take risks, which all involve weighing alternatives? Why would a perfectly happy triune God even create, especially if he would know even one child would be molested and tortured and killed because he did, much less the many others? When we explain the existence of the universe, our explanation should not be more complex than that which we're trying to explain, nor should our explanation be based on faith, or the writings of ancient superstitious Bronze Age goat-herders.

We might even grant for the sake of argument there is a supernatural force (or being) out there. Then at best all Marshall can reasonably conclude is that a god exists, but he has no way to exclude other god-hypotheses, like God ceasing to exist when creating the universe as his last dying act. Or if God still exists, he cannot reasonably determine if God is good or a trickster god, or one who is watching us with enjoyment like rats in a maze to see what we conclude about it all. At best theistic arguments lead us to a distant god, one that is indistinguishable from none at all—an unnecessary hypothesis we can simply do without.

Much more effort needs to be done in order to establish Marshall's God afterward. In order to do this, the evidence for miracles in the distant ancient superstitious past must be able to convince other theists. Yet other theists disagree over where the evidence leads. They are just as skeptical of other religious miracles as I am of them all.

Consider the 800-page book by Michael Alter, *The Resurrection: A Critical Inquiry*.[1] It's the best book of its kind, an encyclopedic refutation of the resurrection of Jesus hypothesis, and it's only Part 1 of a projected 2 volume work. The kicker is that it's not written by an atheist. It's written by a believer, a theist, just not Marshall's kind of theist. He's an Orthodox Jew. And my guess is that no one here tonight who is a Christian will ever read it, or books like it, because your brain will convince you not to do so. You only want to read what confirms your faith so you can stay within the safety net of your social grouping.

Take the Jews of Jesus' day. They believed in Yahweh, that he performed miracles, and they knew their Old Testament prophecies. Yet the overwhelming majority of them did not believe Jesus was raised from the

---

[1] Alter, Michael J. (2015), *The Resurrection: A Critical Inquiry*, Xlibris.

dead by Yahweh. Since these Jews were there and didn't believe, why should we? No, really. Why should we? Why should anyone? The usual answer is that these Jews didn't want to believe because Jesus was not their kind of Messiah, a king who would throw off Roman rule. But then, where did they get that idea in the first place? They got it from their own scriptures. And who supposedly penned them? Yahweh.

Christians will also claim God needed the Jews to make sure Jesus was crucified to atone for our sins, just as he needed Judas to betray him. I myself am baffled as to why an omniscient God could not think of any other way to make this happen. But because he couldn't, God apparently needed to mislead the Jews about the nature of the Messiah. So due to this loving and wise plan of his, Christians have also been given a reason to persecute torture and kill Jews throughout the centuries for their alleged crime of being Christ-killers [the Romans are actually the guilty ones]. Not only this, but the overwhelming majority of Jews will go to hell where Judas is waiting for them. If anyone was sacrificed for the sins of the world it would be the Judas and the Jews. Does this sound fair for a perfectly good, omniscient judge? Really? Think like an outsider for the first time in your lives!

Given what I've said here, 18th-century German critic Gotthold Lessing put a fine point on the problem of a reasonable faith when he wrote:

> Miracles, which I see with my own eyes, and which I have opportunity to verify for myself, are one thing; miracles, of which I know only from history that others say they have seen them and verified them, are another.

All that Christian apologists have is second-, third-, and fourth-hand conflicting testimony found in completed manuscripts dated in the 4th century CE, which Christians doctored up and included known forgeries. The evidence of the Gospels would be thrown out as unreliable testimony in any reasonable court proceedings.

What we have is a childish fairy tale at best, with a fairy tale god acting in ways that can only be depicted in fairy tales. It's time to become adults in our thinking. No more playing a childish pretend game. Think like scientists instead. Think exclusively in terms of the probabilities. Proportion your assent to the strength of evidence. No more double standards. No more special pleading.

In the rebuttal stage I had the chance to make the following points:

The Moral Argument to the Existence of God

As far as I can tell, the Islamic State could make the same moral argument to the existence of their god, using their own morality, where it's okay to rape women, own slaves, chop off heads and burn people alive. Christians like Wallace Marshall would have to agree with their Moral Argument, but disagree with their morals. However, their morals are used as evidence that their god exists, just as his morals are used as evidence his god exists. So certain kinds of morals lead to certain kinds of gods. Or certain kinds of gods are used to justify certain kinds of morals. Which comes first? I'm as sure as sure can be that the morals come first. Where do believers get their morals from? That's as tricky of a question as it is for me. But I can guarantee you Marshall does not get his morals from the Bible. For if he did, his morals would look much like the morals of the Islamic State. For in the Bible, we see much of the same things, like slavery, holy wars, genocide or ethnic cleansing, and Inquisitions.

Regardless, there is no time in the history of ethics where Marshall could not make this argument based on the morals of his day. He could own slaves, offer up his child to Yahweh or have sex slaves and be heard to argue at the local pub that his god is the source of objective morals. This argument to God from morals is empty rhetoric without any content.

Since morals come first, I think Philosopher Raymond Bradley has produced a good counter-argument. Bradley: "If there are universal objective moral truths, then there is no God of the Bible. He then provides some universal objective moral truths that are counter to biblical morality: 1) "It is morally wrong to deliberately and mercilessly slaughter men, women, and children who are innocent of any serious wrongdoing"; 2) "It is morally wrong to provide one's troops with young women captive with the prospect of their being used as sex slaves"; 3) "It is morally wrong to make people cannibalize their friends and family"; 4) "It is morally wrong to practice human sacrifice, by burning or otherwise"; 5) "It is morally wrong to torture people endlessly for their beliefs." He argues that "if we take these moral principles as objective ones, as Christians themselves do, then since we find them commanded and permitted by the God of the Bible, he does not exist."

Infinity Is Not A Number, So The Kalam Argument Fails

The concept of infinity is not an actual number. It's a placeholder for a number beyond our finite conceptions. To see this, just think of an infinite set of even numbers. Now add to that set an infinite number of odd numbers. By adding an infinite set of odd numbers to the infinite set of even numbers we have not increased the actual numbers in that set. So an actual infinite set of numbers does not exist. We could even subtract all numbers with zeros in them, or the numbers 1-1000, or all prime numbers and more, and still have an infinite set of numbers leftover.

With the Kalam argument, Wallace Marshall's error is in thinking infinity is an actual number.[1] Based on this error he says there cannot be an actual infinite number of past events. Well, of course not. That's because infinity isn't an actual number. Since infinity is not an actual number, we cannot count an infinite number of past events. The way Marshall uses infinity assumes there was a beginning an infinite time ago anyway. The truth is that an infinite timeline necessarily lies outside of our epistemic horizons. But this tells us nothing at all about whether the universe is eternal.

Dr. James Lindsay, a friend of mine who has a Ph.D. in math and wrote the book *Dot, Dot, Dot: Infinity Plus God Equals Folly*,[2] says:[3]

> Eternal cosmologies deny the existence of a beginning. Eternal means no beginning and no end. No first moment. No last moment. In an eternal cosmological model, we have to reckon time only from defined moments, and we can imagine a timeline of infinite length in both directions from any point that we choose. The way we conceive of that is not of a beginning infinitely long before or an end infinitely long after but rather as "there's always an earlier moment than any we describe and always a later moment than any we describe.

---

[1] The Kalam Cosmological Argument is a favorite argument of theists and is usually formulated as follows: Everything that begins to exist needs a cause; the universe began to exist; therefore, the universe needs a cause. Theists make a few extra jumps to argue that the caused for the universe's existence is God. One of the claims that they generally argue is that infinity is mathematically problematic, looking to shut down any theory that involves an eternal universe. For treatment of the Kalam, illustrating its many flaws, see Pearce, Jonathan M.S. (2016),*Did God Crete the Universe from Nothing? Countering William Lane Craig's Kalam Cosmological Argument*, Fareham: Onus Books.

[2] Lindsay, James (2013) *Dot, Dot, Dot: Infinity Plus God Equals Folly*, Fareham: Onus Books,

[3] In personal correspondence.

Now the point isn't that we know the universe is eternal. It's that we don't know that it isn't. The whole point, by definition, of an eternal cosmology is that there is no first moment (i.e., no beginning).

He goes on to say,

> The Kalam is exactly the kind of cosmology we would expect from people who hadn't yet discovered science...It would be absurd if they weren't so embarrassingly serious.

7 - Suffering Makes God's Existence Implausible: Loftus vs David Wood

Christian philosopher James F. Sennett has said:[1] "By far the most important objection to the faith is the so-called problem of evil. I tell my philosophy of religion students that, if they are Christians and the problem of evil does not keep them up at night, then they don't understand it."

I'm arguing against the theistic conception of God, who is believed to be all-powerful, or omnipotent, perfectly good, or omnibenevolent and all-knowing, or omniscient. The problem of evil is an internal one to these three theistic beliefs which is expressed in both deductive and evidential arguments concerning both moral and natural evils. I'm going to hopefully combine all of these elements into a novel approach to the problem.

As I do this, keep in mind what Corey Washington said in a debate with William Lane Craig: "We've got to hold theists to what they say...if they say God is omnibenevolent, God is omnibenevolent, if they say God is omnipotent, God is omnipotent. We can't allow theists to sort of play with these words. They mean what they mean. And if God is omnibenevolent, God will not have any more harm in this world than is necessary for accomplishing...greater goods."

Here's the problem: If God is perfectly good, all-knowing, and all-powerful, then the issue of why there is so much suffering in the world requires an explanation. The reason is that a perfectly good God would be opposed to it, an all-powerful God would be capable of eliminating it, and an all-knowing God would know what to do about it.

So, the extent of intense suffering in the world means for the theist that: either God is not powerful enough to eliminate it, or God does not care enough to eliminate it, or God is just not smart enough to know what to do about it. The stubborn fact of intense suffering in the world means that something is wrong with God's ability, or his goodness, or his knowledge.

---

[1] Sennett, James, *This Much I Know: A Postmodern Apologetic,* an unpublished manuscript.

Many theists believe God set the Israelites free from slavery, but he did nothing for the many people who were born and died as slaves in the American south. These theists believe God parted the Red Sea, but he did nothing about the 2004 Indonesian tsunami that killed a quarter of a million people. Many theists believe God provided manna from heaven, but he does nothing for the more than 40,000 people who starve every single day in the world. Those who don't die suffer extensively from hunger pains and malnutrition all of their short lives. Many theists believe God made an axe head to float, but he allowed the Titanic to sink. Many theists believe God added 15 years to King Hezekiah's life, but he does nothing for children who live short lives and die of leukemia. Many theists believe God restored sanity to Nebuchadnezzar but he does nothing for the many people suffering from schizophrenia and dementia today. Many theists believe Jesus healed people, but God does nothing to stop pandemics which have destroyed whole populations of people. Lethal parasites kill one human being every ten seconds. There are many handicapped people, and babies born with birth defects that God does not heal. As God idly sits by, well over 100 million people were slaughtered in the last century due to genocides, and wars. Well over 100 million animals are slaughtered every year for American consumption alone, while animals viciously prey on each other.

Let me tell you about a man named Robert, who for four and a half years heard cruel voices in his head. The cruelest voice said that Satan was going to force him to murder his daughter. You may say that these voices were all lies and should have been treated as such. If you say that, then you don't understand the horror or schizophrenia. You wholeheartedly believe these voices. He was so convinced Satan was going to force him to murder his daughter, that he fought the urge to commit suicide on a daily basis so he wouldn't be the instrument of his daughter's death. Nothing that he tried helped him either, and he tried it all: exorcisms, repentance from every known sin, medications, and counseling. His wife eventually divorced him in fear he may have been a threat to his daughter, leaving him to live alone in a psychotic state. He's recovered a great deal. But why didn't God care?

Then there's former American slave, Frederick Douglass, who described how his Christian master whipped his aunt right before his young eyes. "He took her into the kitchen, and stripped her from neck to waist. He made her get upon the stool, and he tied her hands to a hook in

68

the joist. After rolling up his sleeves, he commenced to lay on the heavy cowskin, and soon the warm, red blood came dripping to the floor." "No words, no tears, no prayers, from his gory victim, seemed to move his iron heart from its bloody purpose. The louder she screamed, the harder he whipped; and where the blood ran fastest, there he whipped longest. He would whip her to make her scream, and whip her to make her hush; and not until overcome by fatigue, would he cease to swing the blood clotted cowskin." Now, why didn't God ever explicitly condemn slavery? Stories like these could fill several libraries.

I'll begin by assuming for the sake of argument that God exists.

Then why did God create something in the first place? Theists will typically defend the goodness of God by arguing he could not have created a world without some suffering and evil. But what reason is there for creating anything at all? Theists typically respond by saying creation was an expression of God's love. But wasn't God already complete in love? If love must be expressed, then God needed to create, and that means he lacked something. Besides, a perfectly good God should not have created anything at all, if by creating something, anything, it also brought about so much intense suffering. By doing so, he actually reduced the amount of total goodness there is, since God alone purportedly has absolute goodness.

I could end my argument here, but let's say God decided to create something anyway. **Then why didn't God just create a heavenly world?** Theists typically believe that a heaven awaits faithful believers when they die, where there will be no "death, or mourning or crying or pain," where believers will have incorruptible bodies, in a perfect existence. So why didn't God just create such a perfect existence in the first place? If there's free will in heaven without sin, then God could've created such a world. To say God initially did create such a world but that there was an angelic rebellion in it merely places the problem of evil back in time. How is it possible to be in the direct presence of a being that has absolute goodness and unlimited power and still desire to rebel against him? Even if this is possible, why didn't God prevent such a rebellion? Pierre Bayle argued: "One might as well compare the Godhead with a father who had let the legs of his children be broken in order to display before an entire city the skill which he has is setting bones; One might as well compare the Godhead with a monarch who would allow strife and seditions to spring up throughout his kingdom in order to acquire the glory of having put an end to them."

Again, I could end my argument here. But let's say God decided to create a fleshly world anyway. **Then why did God create us with free will?** God shouldn't have given free will to his creatures if by doing so he knew it would lead to intense suffering. The giver of a gift is blameworthy if he gives gifts to those whom he knows will terribly abuse those gifts. Any mother who gives a razor blade to a two-year-old is culpable if that child hurts himself or others with it. If, however, God did not give us free will, then Calvinistic theology must justify why our world brings God more glory than a different world where he decrees from eternity that his creatures all perfectly obey him.

Again, I could end my argument here. But let's say God decided to create a fleshly world with free creatures in it anyway. Then **what is the purpose of creating such a world?** It appears to be a cruel game of hide and seek, where God hides and we must find him, and only the few who find him will be rewarded while the many who don't, are punished when they die. If God has foreknowledge then why didn't he just foreknow who would find him even before creating them, and simply place them in heaven in the first place?...then there'd be no one punished for not finding him. If this world is to teach us the virtues of courage, patience, and generosity in the midst of suffering, then those virtues are irrelevant in a heavenly bliss where there is no suffering or pain.

In any case, God should've had three main moral concerns when creating such a world:

Concern One: *that we don't abuse the freedom God gave us.* God should not allow any genocides like the Holocaust; no Joseph Mengele's who tortured concentration camp prisoners; no atomic bombs that devastated Hiroshima; no gulags, no 9/11s, no Cambodian children stepping on land mines, no Columbine shootings, no Jeffery Dahlmers, no gang rapes, or brutal slavery.

Good mothers give their children more and more freedom to do what they want so long as they are responsible with their freedom. And if children abuse this freedom, their mothers will discipline them by taking away their ability to make these choices. It's that simple. If my mother sat by and did nothing while my older brother beat me to death, and if she had the means to stop him and didn't, then she is morally responsible for letting me die. She could even be considered an accomplice.

God could keep us from abusing our freedom. He could've created us with a stronger propensity to dislike doing wrong just like we have an aversion to drinking motor oil. We could still drink it if we wanted to, but it's nauseating.

God could also implant thoughts into a person's head to prevent him from doing evil; much like in Robert's case above, except these thoughts would be good ones.

God has many other means at his disposal here, if we concede for the moment the existence of this present world: One childhood fatal disease or a heart attack could have killed Hitler and prevented WWII. Timothy McVeigh could have had a flat tire or engine failure while driving to Oklahoma City with that truck bomb. Several of the militants who were going to fly planes into the Twin Towers on 9/11 could've been robbed and beaten by New York thugs (there's utilitarianism at its best).

A poisonous snakebite could've sent Saddam Hussein to an early grave averting the Iraq war before it happened. The poison that Saddam Hussein threw on the Kurds, and the Zyklon-B pellets dropped down into the Auschwitz gas chambers could have simply "malfunctioned" by being miraculously neutralized (just like Jesus supposedly turned water into wine). Sure, it would puzzle them, but there are a great many things that take place in our world that are not explainable. Even if they concluded God performed a miracle here, what's the harm? Doesn't God want us to believe in him?

Concern Two: *that the environment God places us in will not cause us excessive suffering.* God should not allow any pandemics, like the Spanish Influenza of 1918 which killed 20 million people, no tornadoes, no floods, no hurricanes, no earthquakes, no devastating fires, no volcanic eruptions, no lethal parasites, or major diseases like cancer, polio, malaria, pneumonia or AIDS. There should be no poisonous creatures like the brown recluse spider, and no poisonous plants like Yew (eat it and you die within minutes).

If God exists and wants us to believe in him, then he should've made it a priority to prevent religious diversity by clearly revealing himself in this world such that only people who refuse to believe would do so. In this way, he'd prevent all religious wars, Crusades, Inquisitions and witch burnings. There'd be no religiously motivated suicide bombers, no Muslim terrorists, and no kamikaze pilots.

71

If God exists, he should stop all natural disasters too, like the Indonesian tsunami. If God had prevented it, none of us would ever have known he kept it from happening, precisely because it didn't happen. Any person who is supposed to be good would be morally obligated to prevent it, especially if all it took was a "snap" of his fingers to do so. Why didn't God stop it?

If the theist claims natural disasters are the result of sin, then the punishments simply do not fit the crimes. God's purported punishments are barbaric when compared to our own. We simply put criminals in jail. We don't break both arms of an infant because her father lied at the office.

If God allows these disasters for a greater good, what's the greater good here? Any paltry benefits to the victims could've been gained by other means. To say the victims are going to be rewarded in heaven for their suffering can never morally justify why they suffered in the first place, otherwise the final eternal state, even if it's pleasant for them, only compensates them for their sufferings. This same reasoning could justify us torturing anyone, so long as we later compensated them for their sufferings.

If God exists, he should not have created predation in the natural world, either. The amount of creaturely suffering here is atrocious as creatures prey on one another to feed themselves. There is no good reason for this and every reason against it. All creatures should be vegetarians. And in order to be sure there is enough vegetation for us all, God could've reduced our mating cycles and/or made edible vegetation to grow as plenteous as wild weeds do today.

Paul Draper has argued that "the theory of evolution of species by means of natural selection explains numerous facts much better than the alternative hypothesis, that each species of plant and animal was independently created by God." Specifically, Draper argues, "Both pain and pleasure contributes to two central biological goals of individual organisms, namely survival and reproduction." But since God doesn't need the biological usefulness of pain and pleasure in attaining these twin goals, and since God additionally needs good moral reasons for allowing for pain, theism is antecedently more implausible than, say, atheism. This is particularly persuasive when we consider how long sentient animals had to suffer through this evolutionary process before the arrival of humans.

In fact, there is no good reason for God to have created animals at all, especially since theists do not consider them part of any eternal scheme, nor are there any moral lessons that animals need to learn from their sufferings. As a result, William Rowe's argument about a fawn that is burned in a forest fire and left to die a slow death without any human witness is gratuitous evil, plain and simple. It serves no greater good.

The theist may object that by making these changes it might go against the laws of nature and/or upset our fine-tuned ecosystem. However, the theist faces a dilemma here: if God created the laws of nature in the first place, then he could've created a different set of laws, and if he didn't create these laws, then where did they come from? Besides, since this present ecosystem is causing so much intense suffering, the question for the theist is why this ecosystem is more important to God than one without so much suffering that constantly needs divine maintenance. People should matter more to God than a fined tuned ecosystem.

If changing the environment in any of these ways requires some adjustment that does not accord with any known laws of nature, what's the problem? The ordering of the world by general laws "seems nowise necessary" to God, as David Hume argued. The theist typically believes God created the universe out of nothing, and if he can do that, he can do anything in his world. He could even perform one or more perpetual miracles here. As far as the theist knows, the whole world operates by perpetual miracles anyway. Are all things possible with God, or not?

Concern Three: *that our bodies will provide a reasonable measure of wellbeing for us.* I want you to think outside the box here. All that seems to be required for this is that we have rational powers to think and to choose, the ability to express our thoughts, and bodies that will allow us to exercise our choices. So we could've been created much differently...easily.

God could've created all human beings with one color of skin. There has been too much killing, slavery, and wars because we are not one race with one language.

God could've created us with much stronger immune systems such that there would be no pandemics which have decimated whole populations of people. At the very least, he could've given us the knowledge to cure these diseases the day after he created us, but he didn't even do that.

God could've created us with self-regenerating bodies. When we receive a cut, it heals itself over time, as does a sprained ankle, or even a broken bone. But why can't an injured spinal cord be made to heal itself, or an amputated leg grow back in a few weeks? If that's all we experienced in this world we wouldn't know any different.

We find a lot of things in nature that God could've done for us. He could've made us all vegetarians, as I mentioned, given us wings on our backs so we could fly to safety if we fell off a cliff, and gills to keep us from drowning.

Only if the theist expects very little from such a being can he defend what God has done. Either God isn't smart enough to figure out how to create a good world, or he doesn't have the power to do it, or he just doesn't care. These are the logical options.

In response, theists resort to claiming we just cannot fathom God's omniscient ways. But this begs the question, because it assumes God exists. What needs to be shown is that God exists, and the empirical evidence of evil is against this. In addition, the theistic response here cuts both ways. We're told God is so omniscient that we can't understand his purposes, and this is true, we can't begin to grasp why there is so much evil in the world, if God exists. *But if God is as omniscient as claimed, then he should know how to create a better world, especially since we do have a good idea of how he could've created differently.*

One main reason a theist claims to believe in a good God is that the arguments for God's existence outweigh the empirical evidence of evil in the world. But as soon as we study those arguments in any depth, they are less than persuasive. The design argument, for instance, is undermined by the extent of evil in the world.

Besides, these arguments don't lead exclusively to theism or to any particular type of theism either, whether it's Judaism, Islam, or the many branches of Christianity. Choosing between theistic religions depends additionally on historical evidence, usually coming from a pre-scientific and superstitious people, even though practically anything can be rationally denied in history.

The main reason people accept a particular type of theism, or none at all, depends to a very large extent on when and where they were born, called the "accidents of birth." For, if you were born in Saudi Arabia, you would be a Sunni Muslim right now. If you were born in India you'd be a Hindu. If you were born in Japan you'd be a Shintoist, and if you were born in Thailand you'd be a Buddhist. Deny it all you want to, but these are the sociological facts.

In conclusion, I personally think any single one of these problems makes the existence of God implausible, but taken together they are insurmountable obstacles to the belief in the theistic God.

8 – God and Horrendous Suffering

I have included the following chapter, as an introduction to my book God and Horrendous Suffering, to show how preparing for debates can give you the impetus to start forming the content for new projects. God and Horrendous Suffering was released on 2021 and yet the debate with David Wood took place in 2007. A debate in 2007 took 14 years to be developed, added to, and eventually become an anthology about which I am extremely excited. In the following piece, you can clearly see the debate opener forming the core to the chapter, to be fleshed out and improved. For example, the three moral concerns become four.

***

The evidential problem of horrendous suffering is one of the most powerful refutations of the theistic god as can be found: If there's a theistic omni-everything god, who is *omnibenelovent* (or perfectly good), *omniscient* (or all-knowing), and *omnipotent* (or all-powerful), the issue of why there is horrendous suffering in the world requires an explanation. The reason is that a perfectly good god would want to eliminate it, an all-knowing god would know how to eliminate it, and an all-powerful god would be able to eliminate it. So the extent of horrendous suffering means that either god does not care enough to eliminate it, or god is not smart enough to eliminate it, or god is not powerful enough to eliminate it. The stubborn fact of horrendous suffering means something is wrong with god's goodness, his knowledge, or his ability.

Just think of this in terms of who has the greatest moral obligation to help someone who is suffering. It's the person who knows of the suffering, who cares the most to alleviate it, and who has the greatest ability to alleviate it. Therefore, the person who has the greatest obligation to alleviate horrendous suffering is a theistic omni-god, if he exists. Anyone who is wholly good would be morally obligated to prevent horrendous suffering, especially if all it took was a "snap" of the fingers.

There are two categories of horrendous suffering that must be adequately explained by apologists for God: 1) *Moral evils* (that is, suffering caused by the choices of moral agents). Examples include: the Holocaust, the atomic obliteration of Hiroshima and Nagasaki, terrorist be-headings, childhood molestation, torture, slavery, gang rapes, wars, and so on. Then there's 2) *Natural evils* (that is, suffering caused by natural disasters). Examples include: pandemics, tsunamis, hurricanes, tornadoes, volcanic eruptions, droughts, earthquakes, massive wildfires, and so on, including the enormous suffering caused by "the kill or be killed" law of predation in the animal kingdom.

There are several levels of suffering stretching from mere hunger pangs to the horrors of the Holocaust. But we don't need to determine the exact demarcation point when the suffering becomes too horrific for an omni-everything god. For the greater the suffering is then the greater the problem of evil is for an omni-god. My focus is on horrendous suffering, the kind that turns our stomachs. It's the best kind of suffering to test the probability of a good god. If believers cannot solve this problem except by focusing on hypothetical possibilities rather than on probabilities, or by punting to ignorance—by saying "God's ways are above ours"—then that god has allowed more suffering in the world than is reasonable for reasonable people to accept. Surely a god who created reasonable people should provide what reasonable people need if he wants us to believe.

If we think exclusively in terms of probabilities, the more horrendous suffering that exists then the less probable an omni-everything god exists, and there is too much horrendous suffering for god to exist! In legal terms, the theistic omni-god should easily be convicted of the crime of *depraved indifference*. This is when a defendant's conduct is "so wanton, so deficient of concern, so lacking in regard for the lives of others, and so blameworthy that it warrants the same criminal liability imposed upon the person who intentionally causes the crime."[1]

The strength of the problem of horrendous suffering depends on one's religious views. It's much greater for *evangelicals* who believe in a god who inspired the horrific tales in the Bible, including sending people into an eternal conscious torment in hell. So apologists like William Lane Craig

---

[1] "Depraved Indifference Law and Legal Definition," *USLegal*, https://definitions.uslegal.com/d/depraved-indifference (Accessed 05/12/2022).

have said, "The problem of evil is certainly the greatest obstacle to belief in the existence of God. When I ponder both the extent and depth of suffering in the world, whether due to man's inhumanity to man or to natural disasters, then I must confess that I find it hard to believe that God exists."[1] Apologist James Sennett echoed what Craig said: "By far the most important objection to the faith is the so-called problem of evil. I tell my philosophy of religion students that if they are Christians and the problem of evil does not keep them up at night, then they don't understand it."[2] The strength of this problem is perhaps the greatest for *Calvinists* who believe in theological determination, as opposed to non-Calvinists who believe in free will.

But every believer faces this problem. Pantheists believe suffering is an illusion (or maya) but they cannot avoid suffering throughout their lives. For *polytheists* their multiple gods aren't powerful enough to decisively overcome suffering, and are believed to cause much of it. *Process theologians* like John Cobb and David Griffin believe their god can't force free-willed agents to do good. Their god can only *persuade* people to do good. But given the fact of horrendous suffering, such a god is shown to be useless in the face of natural disasters, and powerless when it comes to the choices of liars, thieves, molesters, rapists, kidnappers, and killers who refuse to be persuaded. For *protest theologians* like John Roth, god's continual inaction must mean God is directly responsible for the suffering in the world. Their response should be to protest the lack of divine action in hopes that publicly shaming him will goad God into doing good. For *deists*, suffering has little force, but only because they already admit their god is an absentee slum landlord of a world that should be condemned as unsafe for habitation. Then there are *Misotheists* who hate God (from the Greek word *miseo* "to hate"). Their view is a moral position not a stance on the existence of a god. For them it's immoral to praise and worship any moral monster, including a divine one, real or conceptually held in the minds of believers. So scorn, mockery, and rebellion against religious authorities are the appropriate responses. By contrast, for *atheists* who don't believe any god exists, the fact of horrendous suffering is not an intellectual problem at all. Suffering, even

---

[1] Craig, William Lane (2021), "The Problem of Evil." *Reasonable Faith,* https://www.reasona blefaith.org/writings/popular-writings/existence-nature-of-god/the-problem-of-evil/ Accessed (12/11/2021)

[2] Sennett, James, *This Much I Know: A Postmodern Apologetic,* an unpublished manuscript.

horrendous suffering, is what we expect to find in a world that evolved by natural selection.

Let's turn now to consider four moral concerns that an omni-god should have considered when creating a world. Suppose a perfectly good deity exists who didn't need or want anything, yet decided for some mysterious or egotistical reason to create a world to test free creatures. Okay? Then such a deity should have four moral concerns.

Moral Concern One: *The first moral concern for God would be that we don't abuse the freedom given to us.*

The giver of a gift is blameworthy if he or she knowingly gives gifts to people who will terribly abuse them. Any parent who gives a razor blade to a two-year-old is culpable if that child hurts himself or others with it. Good parents give their children more and more freedom to do what they want so long as they are responsible with their freedom. If children abuse their freedom parents will discipline them by taking away their freedom to make bad choices. It's that simple.

Furthermore, children shouldn't have to suffer Draconian kinds of suffering for their actions when they err. When my children misbehaved, I didn't send a proverbial hurricane their way. In fact, as a parent I sought to protect them as much as I could from the severe consequences of their actions. A little pain was a good thing so they could learn from their mistakes. But no caring father would let his children suffer the full brunt of their mistakes, certainly not broken bones or being beaten within an inch of their lives. If a father sat by and did nothing while his children suffered horrendous consequences for their misdeeds, the father is morally culpable for letting it happen. They would certainly want all predators, killers, and rapists locked in jails and prisons away from their children. Since God doesn't do this in our world he is not even as loving as a parent.

An omni-god should have kept us from abusing our freedom by creating us with a stronger propensity to dislike wrongdoing just like we have an aversion to drinking motor oil. We could still drink it if we wanted to, but it's nauseating. Such a deity could easily keep a person from molesting a child or raping someone if at the very thought of it, the person began to suffer severe nausea. We have the ability to do this with alcoholics when it comes to drinking, so it shouldn't be a problem for a good deity to do this with the most heinous of crimes.

80

Nothing of value to God would be lost by him doing so. Since God supposedly can read our minds he can still judge our character by our intentions alone. After noting our intentions to do harm, God could implant good thoughts into our heads to prevent us from actually carrying out our bad intentions.

An omni-god has many other means at his disposal to keep us from harming others. A heart attack could have killed Hitler and prevented WWII. Timothy McVeigh could have had a flat tire or engine failure while driving to Oklahoma City to blow up the Murrah Federal Building and the people in it. The militants who flew planes into the Twin Towers on 9/11 could have been robbed and beaten by New York thugs before they could do so (there's utilitarianism at its best!). A poisonous snakebite could have sent Saddam Hussein to an early grave, averting the Iraq war before it happened. The Zyklon B pellets dropped down into the Auschwitz gas chambers could have simply "malfunctioned" by being miraculously neutralized (just like Jesus supposedly turned water into wine).

Moral Concern Two: *The second moral concern for God would be that the environment he placed us in will not cause us excessive suffering.*

At the very minimum, an omni-god should prevent all natural disasters. If such a god exists the 2004 Indonesian tsunami that killed approximately a quarter million people should never have taken place. If God had prevented it with a miracle, by stopping the underwater earthquake *before it happened*, no one would have been the wiser, precisely because it didn't happen. By doing so, God could have remained hidden, for some hidden reason. Then with a perpetual miracle he could keep it from happening in the future. Such a god could stop all naturally caused horrendous suffering in this manner, and none of us would be the wiser. We would just conclude this is how the natural world works, with much less suffering in it.

An omni-god should not have created predation in the animal world, either. The amount of animal suffering is atrocious, as creatures prey on one another to feed themselves. The extent of animal suffering cries out against the existence of a good god. This horrific suffering is perhaps the most difficult problem of all. To say these creatures do not feel pain is to reject the overwhelming evidence of evolution that proves we are all related as creatures. In lieu of this, an omni-god should have created all living things as vegans like herbivores such as rabbits, deer, sheep, cows, and Hippos. And in order to be sure there is enough vegetation for all of us, God could have reduced our mating cycles and/or made edible vegetation like apple trees, corn stalks, blueberry bushes, wheat, and tomato plants grow as plenteous as wild weeds do today.

An all-powerful god didn't even have to create us such that we needed to eat anything at all. Since theists believe their god can do miracles, he could sustain us all with miraculously created nutrients inside our biological systems throughout our lives, and we wouldn't know anything different. Such a deity could simply do a perpetual miracle here as well. In fact, there is nothing prohibiting God from feeding us by the process of photosynthesis, just like plant life, thereby not requiring animals at all. Given that God didn't do this, many animals are farmed for human consumption under horrible conditions in intensive factory farms, abused in experimental labs, or trapped in horrible ways without any condemnations of animal abuse in god's so-called revelation in the Bible.[1]

Moral Concern Three: *The third moral concern for God would be that our bodies provide a reasonable measure of well-being.*

All that seems to be necessary for God and his plan of salvation is that we have rational powers to think and to choose, the ability to express our thoughts, and bodies that will allow us to exercise our choices. So we could have been created much much differently.

An omni-god should have created all human beings with one color of skin. There, that was easy! There has been too much institutional racism, race-based slavery, and too many tribalistic wars because we don't all have the same color of skin. Such a deity should also have made all creatures capable of sexually self-reproducing, like zebra sharks, Komodo dragons, some reptiles, and other species. If God had done this it would eliminate gender discrimination and gay hate crimes, since there wouldn't be any gender or sexual differences between us.

An omni-god should have created us with much stronger immune systems so there would be no pandemics that decimate whole populations,

---

[1] See Loftus, John W. (2014), *Christianity is Not Great,* Amherst: Prometheus, for a fairly exhaustive discussion of these Biblical passages.

or chronic diseases like cancer, emphysema, leukemia, or for that matter, babies born with deformed limbs, blindness, deafness, dumbness, and so on. This is horrific suffering that God should never have created, or used as any sort of punishment for our misdeeds, or allowed for any good overarching mysterious purpose.

Such a god could have created us with self-regenerating bodies. When we receive a cut, it heals itself over time, as does a sprained ankle or even a broken bone. But why can't an injured spinal cord heal itself? Why can't an amputated leg grow back in a few weeks? If that's all we experienced in this world we wouldn't know any different. Many animals can regrow new parts of their bodies to replace those parts that have been damaged. Lizards can grow new tails. Sharks continually replace lost teeth. Spiders can regrow missing legs. An octopus can regrow severed arms. Starfish can regrow new arms and even grow an entirely new body out of a severed arm.

We find lots of examples in nature that an omni-god could have created in us but didn't. Such a god could have created us with a much higher threshold of pain. He could have given us fish-like gills to keep us from drowning. He could have given us wings on our backs so we could fly to safety if we fell off a cliff. Or, he could have made us much smaller in size so if we accidentally fell off that cliff we wouldn't get hurt, just like ants who have a very low terminal velocity.

Moral Concern Four: *A fourth moral concern for God would be to prevent a wide diversity of religions in the world.*

If there is an omni-god he should have made it a priority to prevent religious diversity by clearly revealing himself in this world such that only people who consciously refuse to believe would do so. There would be no such thing as reasonable non-belief in the one true sect-specific religion, regardless of when and where we were born, or how we might be culturally indoctrinated otherwise. Such a god would have made his revelation available to every culture and buttressed it with some astounding evidence-based miracles. This deity would provide a naturalistic moral code for everyone that excluded all religions that were misogynistic, racist, homophobic, nationalistic, and otherwise barbaric. In this way, he'd prevent religiously motivated wars, crusades, inquisitions, witch burnings, suicide bombers, and terrorists. Given the horrendous suffering caused by religious diversity, the probability that an omni-god exists is inversely proportional to the amount of religious diversity that exists, and there is way too much of it to suppose he does.[1]

To sum up so far, given these four moral concerns it is crystal clear that a god who created this world just doesn't care about us. God had a reckless disregard for our safety by giving us the gift of freedom before we could use it responsibly, he placed us in an environment that causes us excessive suffering, and gave us bodies that don't provide a reasonable measure of well-being, without letting us know which religion is true from a great diversity of religions.

Only if theists expect very little from their divine being can they defend what their god has done. Either their god is not smart enough to figure out how to create a good world, or God doesn't have the power to create it, or God just doesn't care. You pick. These are the options given this world.

Four Apologetic Strategies:

Marilyn McCord Adams admits that "the standard apologetic strategies for 'solving' the problem of evil are powerless in the face of horrendous evils."[2] When it comes to animal suffering C.S. Lewis admitted that, "the Christian explanation of human pain cannot be extended to animal pain. So far as we know beasts are incapable either of sin or virtue: therefore, they can neither deserve pain nor be improved by it."[3]

Still, there are four apologetic strategies used in solving the problem of horrendous suffering. I call them excuses.

According to one excuse, God won't help us since he's more interested in building our character, and horrendous suffering builds character.

This is one of the least successful strategies for answering the problem. Suffering is one thing. Horrendous suffering is another. We're talking about the supposed value horrific suffering produces for the very people who suffer, not any hindsight lessons for future generations.

---

[1] Religious diversity is the problem I seek to solve in my 2013 book, *The Outsider Test for Faith,* Amherst: Prometheus.
[2] Adams, Marilyn & Adams, Robert Merrihew (1990, eds.), *The Problem of Evil*, New York: Oxford University Press, p. 212.
[3] Lewis, C.S. (1962), *The Problem of Pain*, New York: Macmillan, p. 129.

It's also improbable that the virtues we learn in this world, such as compassion for the poor, patience in times of turmoil, forgiveness for someone who has wronged us, and the like, will even be needed in a heavenly bliss where there is no pain or suffering for which to have compassion, patience, or to grant forgiveness.

I am a white male who is not butt ugly (or so a few people tell me), who grew up in a middle-class family with all the privileges that entails. I have never spent a night in a hospital bed so far, nor have I gone hungry. I have had my wits about me (most of the time anyway). Yet life has been hard for me. This life has tried me to the core without experiencing any horrendous suffering in it. So this world doesn't need it if my life is any indication. All that a good god must do is to eliminate the horrendous kinds of suffering in our lives. There is plenty of suffering left in this life to challenge us.

A second excuse used by apologists is that God can't help us when free will is involved, or he cannot help us very much. God needs to let our free choices play themselves out.

But as it stands theists are the first ones to say unrestricted freedom is not a good thing. In the case of heinous crimes, we put criminals in prison. We do not let them roam the streets once they are discovered. They lose their freedom in the interests of having a safe society. Safety is a higher value than freedom. The theistic god has a mixed-up sense of what is more valuable, for that god thinks human freedom is more valuable than having a safe society.

All of us have a very limited range of free choices anyway, if we have any at all. The limits of our choices are set by our genetic material and our environment. It does absolutely no good at all to have free will and not also have the ability to exercise it. Some people don't have the strength needed to stop an attacker, while others don't have the rational capacity needed to spot a con-artist. I could not be a world-class athlete even if I wanted to. Our free will to do what we want is limited by our age, race, gender, mental capacity, financial means, and geographical locality. Since we already have limited choices then God should further limit our choices if we seek to cause horrific harm to others.

A third excuse is that God cannot do away with horrendous suffering because suffering is a necessary by-product of causal natural laws. To have the one is to have the other.

85

However, the apologist believes God created the universe from nothing, along with the laws of nature. So, if God can do that, he can also create a different universe with different laws of nature without any horrendous suffering in it. It just doesn't make any sense that God chose to create this world with so much horrific suffering, when he could've created a better one without it.

Even if God failed to create a good universe initially, he could still do miracles in this world to correct any errors in it. An omnipotent miracle-working god can do anything in the material universe, or he's not a miracle-working god. Even apologist Richard Swinburne agrees: "God is not limited by the laws of nature; he makes them and he can change or suspend them—if he chooses."[1] In a 2003 debate on the existence of God, Swinburne said "God could have made bodies repel each other" or "raise this stadium into the air." However, all god does in today's world is to imprint an image of Jesus on a potato chip!

Since this world is causing so much horrific suffering the question for the theist is why the laws of this world are fixed and necessary when God could intervene to alleviate the most horrific kinds of suffering. If changing the world requires some miraculous adjustment what's the problem? People should matter enough for God to do that. I wonder if theists have really thought through the implications of a god who prefers this present set of natural laws with its sufferings over constant miraculous maintenance. Does their god care? Is their god lazy?

When apologists defend the miracles in the Bible and elsewhere, they will talk about an omnipotent god who created the world out of nothing, who sent fire down from the sky, and parted a sea that allowed six million Hebrews to pass on dry ground, who lived in the desert for forty years where their sandals never wore out, and were fed by manna from heaven. An omnipotent god can do anything they'll say. It even says so in Matthew 19:26: "With God all things are possible." Their god is a miracle-working god. So it shouldn't be difficult to believe god does miracles, they'll add. Yet when it comes to alleviating horrendous suffering, they argue God can't do that. Full Stop. **This is nothing less than intellectual dishonesty!**

---

[1] Swinburne, Richard (1997), *Is There a God?*, Oxford: Oxford University Press, as quoted in Dawkins, Richard (2007), *The God Delusion,* London: Black Swan, p. 58.

I maintain that the burden of proof is upon apologists to show why any of my suggested changes to the world are improbable for an omnipotent miracle-working god. Nothing short of this will do. I am suggesting there are several things an omni-god could do to eliminate horrendous suffering without producing a chaotic world, or inhibiting our character development, that would help draw us to him, all of which are easy to conceive and already found in the animal kingdom. **Since God could have done differently but did not, he is to blame for all horrific suffering in this world.**

A fourth excuse used by apologists is to punt to mystery by claiming we simply cannot understand god's reasons for allowing horrendous suffering in this world.

The truth is that it seems very likely we should be able to see god's reasons for allowing it, since most theists also claim God wants us to believe in him, and will condemn us in the afterlife if we don't. More importantly, this answer cuts both ways. We're told we can't understand god's purposes, and this is true. We can't begin to grasp why there is so much suffering in our world if a good omnipotent god exists. But if God is omniscient as claimed, he should know how to create a better world, especially since we do have a good idea how he could've created it.

So which is more likely, that we cannot begin to understand god's omniscient ways, or that we can have some kind of idea about them? If we consider the idea that we're all created in god's image the answer seems obvious. We should indeed have some kind of idea about god's omniscient ways. Since this is so, and since we have good ideas on how God might have done things differently, the most reasonable conclusion by far, is that an all-powerful, omniscient, perfectly-good god does not exist.

Conclusion

If you name any specific example of horrendous suffering in this world, I can show you how an omni-god could have eliminated it, which would still leave plenty of suffering for an omni-god to test us in this world, if that's important to a god who can predict what we will do anyway.

In order to evade this challenge of mine I have found Christian apologists to be experts at cherry picking god's supposed divine attributes of omnipotence, omniscience, and omnibenevolence, depending on the problem to be solved.

When it comes to god's *omnipotence,* apologists embrace this attribute when it comes to him creating an unfathomable and mysterious universe that continually surprises us. But when it comes to horrendous suffering, apologists conveniently negate it by claiming we cannot understand god's unfathomable and mysterious ways. God, like a father, knows best, they say. One apologist, Thomas Oord, has even argued that God cannot interfere in the world he created, or with free willed choices intent on doing harm. According to him, God simply doesn't intervene in the world.[1]

How do apologists know this? They don't. They just affirm it because of the need to believe. So in order to save their faith from refutation they must allow god's omnipotence to only go so far, and no farther. This is where god's power arbitrarily ends, where the apologist needs it to end to solve a problem for faith.

When it comes to god's *omniscience* apologists embrace this attribute when it comes to God reading our minds, hearing billions of prayers at the same time, and knowing everything that can be known, including minute details into the distant future billions of years from now. But when it comes to horrendous suffering, apologists negate it by claiming God didn't know how to create a good world without animals, or without natural disasters, or one in which free-willed creatures do no harm. Many apologists, such as William Hasker and Greg Boyd, have come to embrace Open Theism which denies that God can foreknow free-willed human actions so their god isn't to be blamed for what we do.

How do apologists know this? They don't. They just affirm it because of the need to believe. So in order to save their faith from refutation they must allow god's omniscience to only go so far, and no farther. This is where god's knowledge arbitrarily ends, where the apologist needs it to end, to solve a problem for faith.

When it comes to god's *omnibenevolence,* apologists embrace this attribute when it comes to God love in sending his son Jesus to pay the ultimate price by dying a horrible death for our sins. But when it comes to suffering, apologists like Michael Peterson, and Bruce Little, they negate it

---

[1] Oord, Thomas Jay (2019), *God Can't: How to Believe in God and Love after Tragedy, Abuse, and Other Evils*, Grasmere, ID: SacraSage Press.

by claiming God does not care that much about our daily lives. In their view, God does not care enough to "micromanage" the world. So they triumphantly proclaim god is off the hook for much of the suffering we experience in the world.

How do apologists know this? They don't. They just affirm it because of the need to believe. So in order to save their faith from refutation they must only allow god's omnibenevolence to only go so far, and no farther. This is where god's omni-benevolence arbitrarily ends, where the apologist needs it to end, to solve a problem for faith.

If this is not their point, then what is it? Certainly, an omniscient god knows how to intervene. Certainly, an omnipotent god has the ability to do so. Shouldn't an omnibenevolent god have the motivation to do so?

So the evidential problem of horrendous suffering is one of the most powerful refutations of the classical theistic god as can be found.

9 – God of Genocide: A Debate. Loftus vs Randal Rauser

There's so much divinely caused and commanded violence in the Bible it can be said that the fear of an angry punishing God is its most prevalent theme, hands down. From the irrational and horrific punishments in the Garden of Eden, to the irrational and horrific punishments predicted in the book of Revelation, and everything in between, we see an angry, cruel, and barbaric god. That's his usual mode of operation. If people obeyed, they were rewarded. But woe to people who didn't obey.

No wonder serious biblical scholars argue that the god of the Bible is modeled after ancient kings, who were themselves often cruel towards their own subjects. God is just like what we find in the story of Job. Job was a good man but God destroyed everything he had, and killed all his sons, daughters and servants, just to win a bet with Satan. Such a wanton disregard toward a human being is utterly reprehensible and barbaric. Kings could do that. But a perfectly good god should not do it.

Tonight, everything hinges on Rauser's moral intuitions. His moral intuitions cause him to believe in two contrary irreconcilable propositions. On the one hand, he believes the Bible uniquely and unmistakably reveals the actions and commands of God. On another hand, he rejects the violence in the Bible which uniquely and unmistakably reveals a cruel god.

To accomplish this feat, Rauser offers a scenario to show we can sometimes trust our intuitions, despite the lack of objective evidence. He asks us to consider a man who sincerely believed he was innocent of a crime even though all the objective evidence pointed to his guilt. Rauser claims the man is in a position to know he's innocent because he personally knows that he's innocent, even if the objective evidence points to him. So let's picture this. There are several eyewitnesses along with video footage of the man killing someone with a gun he had purchased the day before, which was found at the scene of the crime with his fingerprints on it. With this objective evidence the man should honestly accept that he has a serious case of amnesia, or been drugged, hypnotized, or even lobotomized. He is guilty beyond a reasonable doubt.

I think there is a psychological reason Rauser uses this particular analogy. It's because he is that man! He's the one who, as an apologist, must defend the existence and goodness of an imaginary deity at all costs, despite the overwhelming objective evidence to the contrary. The very fact he uses such an absurd analogy is a tacit admission that the needed objective evidence does not exist.

The reason Rauser maintains the Bible is the divinely inspired revelation of a good God isn't because of the texts in the Bible. It's because he imagines himself communicating with a divine friend who only exists in his head. He should love singing the lyrics in the worship Hymn, In the Garden: "And he walks with me and he talks with me and he tells me I am his own." In crass terms, Rauser is the sophisticated counter-part to a babbling bum who seems to be talking to someone else as he walks down the street. I mean no offense. Rauser has a brilliant mind. It's just used in defense of the absurd.

But what exactly are moral intuitions? On my view they mainly stem from empathy, the ability to understand and share the feelings of others as equal persons who are deserving of respect, dignity, sympathy and compassion. Once we stop viewing and treating other people as non-persons and view them with dignity and of equal value, we are able to be decent human beings, kind people, compassionate neighbors, loving citizens, and global humanitarians. Upon realizing this we inevitably will reject the Bible with its god as a product of an ancient barbaric era. There is no rescuing the god of the Bible, since that god was created by ancient barbaric people. What we have in the Bible are the codified ethics of the moral "intuitions" of ancient people. It's time to be consistent by rejecting the Bible and its god in total.

If Rauser still wants to talk in terms of moral intuitions he should question several important Christian beliefs of his. He should reject the Adam & Eve story as reprehensible, in what's best described as the mere quest for knowledge by the first pair of humans. Yet God punished them, along with every sentient being from the beginning of time, with all the suffering this world has ever experienced. Furthermore, he should reject the belief that our sins make us deserving of intense agony forever in hell. He should also reject the belief that a completely pure and innocent person needed to die a horrific death on the cross to atone for our sins, punished as he was, in such a gruesome way by such a kind loving god. *Cough* Rauser should reject his belief that his god only saves people who accept Jesus by faith into their lives--including the death-bed conversions of sex traffickers, drug lords, and Mafia hit men--rather than saving good kind decent loving people.

In Rauser's book, Jesus Loves Canaanites: Biblical Genocide in the Light of Moral Intuition, he talks about The Jesus Principle. This intuitive moral principle allows him to deny that God commanded the Canaanite genocide. He writes: "The Jesus Principle is predicated on the assumption that Jesus is the final and ultimately authoritative locus of divine revelation. As a result, Jesus provides the final guide for all interpretation and application."

Really? Let's take a look.

Before we do, I would find it strange if Rauser didn't accept the authority of Paul, the most important apostle of Jesus. While Jesus doesn't explicitly affirm the Canaanite genocide, Paul does. When preaching in Antioch he said: "The God of Israel chose our fathers... and made them great in the land of Egypt, and led them out of it, and when he had destroyed seven nations in the land of Canaan, he gave them their land as an inheritance. (Acts 13:16-19).

The Epistle to the Hebrews also affirms the Canaanite genocide. In the famous faith chapter, it praises Rahab the prostitute's faith, who helped the Israelites destroy the city of Jericho by hiding two men who had been sent to spy on the city (11:30-31).

This includes killing witches (Ex. 22:18), heretics (Deut. 13:12-19), homosexuals (Lev. 18:22, 20:13), people who work on the Sabbath Day (Ex. 31:14-15, 35:2), people who commit bestiality (Ex. 22:19), adulterers (Lev. 20:10), false prophets (Deut. 13:5), and children who insult or strike their parents (Ex. 21:15, 17).

Back to Jesus, leading up to the shocking conclusion.

Jesus affirmed the truth and permanence of every letter of the law. In Luke 16:17 Jesus said, "It is easier for heaven and earth to pass away than for one letter of the Law to become void." [see also Matthew 5:17-20.] In saying this, Jesus affirmed all the laws of the Hebrew God Yahweh, who always seems to be threatening violence, committing violence, and commanding violence upon others.

Jesus also affirmed three morally atrocious biblical stories.

1) Jesus Affirmed the Genocidal Story of Noah:

Matthew 24:37-41: "As it was in the days of Noah, so it will be at the coming of the Son of Man. For in the days before the flood, people were eating and drinking, marrying and giving in marriage, up to the day Noah entered the ark; and they knew nothing about what would happen until the flood came and took them all away."

2) Jesus Affirmed the Genocidal Story of Sodom and Gomorrah:

Luke 17:28-30: "On the day that Lot went out from Sodom it rained fire and brimstone from heaven and destroyed them all."

Matthew 11:23-24: "I say to you that it will be more tolerable for the land of Sodom in the day of judgment, than for you." [See 2 Peter 2:5-9].

Now for the shocking conclusion.

3) Jesus Affirmed Honor Killings by Stoning:

The Pharisees accused Jesus of being too lenient in his observance of the law. So Jesus counterpunches them in Mark 7:9-12: "You have a fine way of setting aside the commands of God in order to observe your own traditions! For Moses said, 'Honor your father and mother,' and, 'Anyone who curses their father or mother is to be put to death.' But you say that if anyone declares that what might have been used to help their father or mother is Corban (that is, devoted to God) then you no longer let them do anything for their father or mother." (NIV)

Corban is an Aramaic word that refers to a sacrifice, oath, or gift to God. The Pharisees allowed for this loophole so someone could make an oath to offer a gift to the temple, like one would set up a trust fund, in order to avoid giving it for the care of one's aging parents.

Jesus' first scriptural quote to "Honor your father and mother" is one of the Ten Commandments. Jesus' second scriptural quote that "Anyone who curses (literally dishonors) their father or mother is to be put to death", is found in Ex. 21:17 and Lev. 20:9. Jesus says the Corban loophole sets aside these two commands of God. For such a son would be disobeying a direct command of God by dishonoring his parents, while the Pharisees would be disobeying God's command by not putting him to death.

Deuteronomy 21:18-21 elaborates (i.e., the second law): "If someone has a stubborn and rebellious son who does not obey his father and mother and will not listen to them when they discipline him, his father and mother shall take hold of him and bring him to the elders at the gate of his town. They shall say to the elders, 'This son of ours is stubborn and rebellious. He will not obey us. He is a glutton and a drunkard.' Then all the men of his town are to stone him to death."

In this, Jesus is affirming the Old Testament law of honor killings by stoning, for only if both of the laws Jesus cites are to be obeyed can his analogy succeed, that the Pharisees have set aside the laws of God in order to observe their traditions.

Rauser is therefore impaled on the horns of a dilemma. Give up The Jesus Principle or give up your moral intuitions. You can't have it both ways.

Rauser claims both that God was accommodating his commands to their hardened hearts, and/or that God was progressively leading believers to civilized notions about morality down through the centuries. Hindsight justifications like those can only mean God's revelation in the Bible is indistinguishable from him not revealing anything at all. If God cannot do better than that, he might as well be dead to us.

10 – Was Jesus Born of a Virgin? Loftus vs William Albrecht

My debate opponent believes a virgin named Mary gave birth to a divine child named Jesus over two-thousand years ago. The most significant problem is that theologians cannot explain how a human being and a god can be one and the same, that is, 100% human and 100% divine, with every essential characteristic of humanity and divinity included. How can a god be a god if he has a body? How can an infinite timeless god exist in time? Conversely, how can a human be a human if he or she doesn't have a body? How can a finite human take on eternal godlike characteristics and still remain a human being? How can a human be perfectly good incapable of being tempted to sin, and yet also be tempted to sin? Christians themselves have shown the incoherence of a divine/human being by their 2000-year long disagreements over it.

Make no mistake about it. This is what my debate opponent is aiming at in this debate. The virgin birth is a first step toward claiming Jesus was God incarnate. My aim is to stop him short of this first step, even though his case isn't done until he tackles the second step by dealing with some formidable philosophical objections to a divine/human being. With no such being, there's no virgin birth either.

Let's start by talking about the kind of evidence we need.

All claims about the objective world require sufficient objective evidence appropriate to the nature of the claim. This applies to ordinary claims, extraordinary claims and miraculous claims. The amount and quality of the evidence required are dependent on the type of claim being made.

An ordinary claim is one made about events that are commonplace within nature, which require ordinary levels of evidence. Most all of these claims are based on testimonial evidence alone. That is, the trustworthiness of the person making the claim is enough to establish them, especially where there's no reason to suspect deception and there's no dispute by others as to the facts. [Example: "Earlier today I was in Indiana."]

An extraordinary claim is one made about events that are extremely unusual, rare and even strange within the world of nature. Mere testimonial evidence is helpful but not enough to establish these claims. They require some strong objective evidence for them. That is, the more unusual the claim is then the stronger the objective evidence must be for them. [Example: "I was abducted by an alien"].

A miraculous claim is one made about events that are impossible to take place by natural processes alone, which requires a high level of strong objective evidence for them. As David Hume argued, "No testimony is sufficient to establish a miracle, unless the testimony be of such a kind, that its falsehood would be more miraculous than the fact which it endeavors to establish." The fact that a miracle requires extraordinary evidence over and above the fallibility of ordinary human testimony is not an unreasonable demand. It's the nature of the beast. A forensic TV show I watched had a character say, "The evidence doesn't lie. People do." If this is acknowledged in criminal investigations it should be acknowledged much more so in miraculous investigations. So mere testimonial evidence is insufficient when it comes to miracle claims, especially when it comes to miracle claims in the distant past from sources we cannot cross-examine for consistency and truth.

Tonight, I'm going to show that the required objective evidence for the miraculous birth of Jesus is not there, at all. Beyond this, I'm going to show the testimonial evidence in the New Testament is insufficient. My main point is that if the gospels are inaccurate and untrustworthy in historical matters that we can check, then there's absolutely no reason to think they are accurate and trustworthy when it comes to the miraculous virgin birth of Jesus either.

The most significant problem for my debate opponent is that there's no objective evidence to corroborate the virgin birth stories in the New Testament. None. None at all! Where's the evidence Mary was a virgin? We hear nothing about her wearing a barbaric chastity belt to prove her virginity. No one checked for an intact hymen before she gave birth either. Where's the evidence that neither Joseph nor any other man was the father? Maury Povich was not there with a DNA test to verify Joseph was not the baby's daddy, nor did he test others.

We don't even have firsthand testimonial evidence for it, since the story is related to us by others, not Mary, or Joseph. At best, all we have is the second-hand testimony of one person, Mary, or two if we include Joseph who was unreasonably convinced Mary was a virgin because of a dream, yes, a dream (see Matthew 1:19-24). We never get to independently cross-examine them, along with the people who knew them, which we would need to do, since they may have a very good reason for lying, like a pregnancy out of wedlock! Before there can be a virgin birth one must first show Mary wasn't pregnant. One must also show that neither Joseph nor any other man was the baby's daddy.

What we know is that neither of the two earliest New Testament writers refer to the virgin birth of Jesus. That's very telling. Neither the apostle Paul nor the author of the gospel of Mark referred to it. It's inconceivable neither of them mentioned it. The virgin birth story was an unimportant afterthought for the later gospels of Matthew and Luke. This only makes sense as a non-historical myth made up in hindsight to explain how Jesus came down from the sky above the clouds to the earth.

Additionally, in the gospel of Mark, the family of Jesus themselves thought he was crazy, not God's son. "He is out of his mind," they said, and tried "to take charge of him (Mark 3:19–21, 31–35). This makes no sense if the virgin birth stories are true in the later gospels of Matthew and Luke. How could his mother Mary forget how her son Jesus was conceived, or what was said about him at the time of his birth? The angel Gabriel said he would be called "the Son of God" (Luke 1:35). Her cousin Elizabeth said Mary was the "mother of my Lord" (Luke 1:43), and she herself said, "from henceforth all generations shall call me blessed" (Luke 1:48). No mother would ever forget the circumstances of his birth, if it happened as reported.

In Luke's gospel when Mary first hears from the angel Gabriel that she's to give birth, she objects by saying, "How shall this be, since I know not a man?" (Luke 1:34). Surely Mary wouldn't feel it necessary to inform Gabriel that she hadn't had sex with a man. If this conversation took place at all, she would've said, "How shall this be, since I know not my husband." The way it's written in Luke is to justify Mary's virginity to the reader, rather than to tell us what she said. So Mary's stated objection to the angel is a literary invention.

Now one might simply trust the anonymous gospel writer(s) who wrote this extraordinary story down, but why? How is it possible that THEY could find out a virgin named Mary gave birth to a deity? No reasonable investigation could take Mary and/or Joseph's word for it. With regard to

Joseph's dream, Thomas Hobbes tells us, "For a man to say God hath spoken to him in a Dream, is no more than to say he dreamed that God spoke to him; which is not of force to win belief from any man." [Leviathan, chap. 32.6] So it's down to unreliable hearsay testimonial evidence from Mary. Why should we believe her? Would you?

It gets worse. There are seven facts to consider.

1) The Genealogies are Inaccurate and Irrelevant. The royal genealogies of Jesus in the later gospels of Luke (3:23–37) and Matthew (1:1–17) have historical problems with them. For instance, Matthew's gospel makes Jesus a descendent of king Jeconiah (1:11), even though the prophet Jeremiah had proclaimed none of Jeconiah's descendants would ever sit of the throne of David (Jer. 22:30). Someone messed up big time here, don't you think?

The genealogies of Jesus are irrelevant if he was born of a virgin. Jewish royal lineages are traced through men and not women, so Luke's genealogy is irrelevant since it traces the lineage of Jesus through Mary.[1] Matthew's genealogy is equally irrelevant, since it traces the lineage of Jesus through Joseph, who was not his father, according to gospel accounts. To desperately claim Mary's baby was a new divine creation unrelated to the lineages of either Mary or Joseph, also makes the genealogies irrelevant. For then it wouldn't matter which mother's womb God decided to create his son inside.

Modern genetics decisively render the genealogies irrelevant since one cannot even have a human being without the genetic contributions of both a male seed and a female egg. To claim, as Catholic New Testament scholar Raymond Brown did, that Jesus was "technically" the adopted son of Joseph, is absurd and also irrelevant since only bloodlines count in royal lineages. Adopted sons would never legitimately inherit any throne.

2) Jesus Was Not Born in Bethlehem. In Matthew 2:5, we're told Jesus was to be born in Bethlehem. But the precise phrase "Bethlehem

---

[1] Many, though not all, Christian apologists harmonize the two contradictory genealogies of Jesus set out in the Gospels of Matthew and Luke by claiming Matthew's is patrilineal and Luke's is matrilineal. See Pearce, Jonathan M.S. (2016), "Conflicting Genealogies of Jesus and the Thesis of a Matrilineal Bloodline Refuted," *A Tippling Philosopher, OnlySky*, https://only sky.media/jpearce/conflicting-genealogies-jesus-thesis-matrilineal-bloodline-refuted/ (Accessed 06/20/2022).

Ephratah" in the original prophecy of Micah 5:2 refers not to a town, but to a family clan: the clan of Bethlehem, who was the son of Caleb's second wife, Ephratah (1 Chron. 2:19, 2:50–51, 4:4). Furthermore, Micah's prophecy predicts a military commander who would rule over the land of Assyria (which never happened), and was certainly not about a future Messiah.

The earliest gospel of Mark begins by saying Jesus came from Nazareth of Galilee, not from Bethlehem (Mark 1:9). Let that sink it. The first gospel says he's from Nazareth. In the later Gospel of John, Jesus was rejected as the Messiah precisely because the people of Nazareth knew he was born and raised in their town! That's the whole reason they rejected him as the Messiah! They rhetorically asked, "How can the Messiah come from Galilee?" They said, "A prophet does not come out of Galilee" (John 7:42, 52). [He was from Nazareth. Therefore, he's not the Messiah.]

Since everyone knew the Messiah would not come from Galilee, Matthew and Luke invented conflicting stories to overcome this insurmountable problem. In Matthew's gospel—the one most concerned with making Jesus fit prophecy—Joseph's family is living in Bethlehem when Jesus was born (Matt. 2). In order to explain how Jesus got to Nazareth, Joseph was warned in a dream to flee to Egypt because of Herod (Matt. 2:15). After Herod died, Joseph took his family to Nazareth and lived there (Matt. 2:21–23). Luke's gospel, by contrast, claims Joseph and Mary lived in the town of Nazareth but traveled to Bethlehem for a Roman census, at which time Jesus was born (Luke 1:26; 2:4). After he was born, they went back home to Nazareth (Luke 2:39).

When we compare Matthew and Luke's accounts, Raymond Brown concludes, "Despite efforts stemming from preconceptions of biblical inerrancy or of Marian piety, it is exceedingly doubtful that both accounts can be considered historical. A review of the implications explains why the historicity of the infancy narratives has been questioned by so many scholars, even by those who do not in advance (i.e., a priori) rule out the miraculous."

To make these stories work they invented a world-wide Roman census (per Luke), to get the holy family to Bethlehem, and the slaughter of the innocents by Herod (per Matthew), to explain why the holy family left Bethlehem for good. Matthew's gospel invented a Messianic Star for emphasis, which was overkill, based on Numbers 24:17. But there was no census, no massacre of children and no Bethlehem star. [As we'll see in the next three facts to consider].

101

3) There Was No Census. Luke's gospel tells us something bizarre, that Joseph had to go to Bethlehem to register for the census because "he was from the house and lineage of David." (Luke 2:4) According to Luke's genealogy, King David had lived forty-two generations earlier. Why should everyone have had to register for a census in the town of one of his ancestors forty-two generations earlier? There would be millions of ancestors by that time, and the whole empire would have been uprooted. Why forty-two generations and not thirty-five, or sixteen? If this requirement was only for the lineage of King David, what was Caesar Augustus thinking when he ordered it? He had a king, Herod.

Both Matthew and Luke said Jesus was born during the time of Herod the Great (Matthew 2:1, Luke 1:5). Herod died in 4 BC, so Jesus was born at the latest in 4 BC. The only known census of that period was a local one in Galilee which took place in 6 AD by Syrian governor Quirinius. There's a gap of ten years between Herod's death and the alleged census, which means there was no census at the birth of Jesus, if he was born during the reign of Herod. But Luke's gospel said it was a world-wide census, not a local one. And that census didn't take place at all, for as Raymond Brown tells: "A census of the known world under Caesar Augustus never happened" and he reigned from 27 BC to 14 AD.

4) There Was No Slaughter of the Innocents. In Matthew's gospel king Herod was said to have ordered all the male children "in Bethlehem and all the surrounding countryside" to be slaughtered (2:16). But there is no other account of such a massacre in any other source. It's clear that the first-century Jewish historian Josephus hated Herod. He chronicled in detail his crimes, many of which were lesser in kind than this alleged wholesale massacre of children. Yet nowhere does Josephus' mention this slaughter even though he was in a position to know of it, and even though he would want to mention it. So the story is a gospel fiction, like the virgin birth story.

5) There Was No Star of Bethlehem. Matthew's gospel says: "The star, which they (the Magi) had seen in the east, went on before them until it came and stopped over the place where the child was." (2:9–10). There is no independent corroboration of this tale by any other source,

Christian or otherwise. No astrologer/astronomer anywhere in the world recorded this event, even though they systematically searched the stars for guidance and predictions of the future. More significantly the author of Luke chose not to include the story of a Star, Magi, or the attempt on Jesus' life, which is telling, since his gospel was written after "a careful study of everything" he says, so readers could know what actually took place from what didn't. (1:1-4).

Theories for this Star include a comet, a supernova, or the conjunction of planets. The fatal problem is that none of them conform to what the text actually says in Matthew's gospel. The Magi see the Star "leading" or directing them to Bethlehem from Jerusalem. Not only are moving stars pre-scientific nonsense, they would be moving in a southern direction, from Jerusalem down to Bethlehem. Stars don't move in the sky, and they certainly don't appear to move in a southerner direction. They all appear to move from the east to west, like the sun, because of the spin of the earth. Then we're told the Star stopped in the sky directly over a place in Bethlehem. But there's no way to determine which specific house a star stopped over, if it did! This is only consistent with pre-scientific notions of the earth being the center of the universe with the stars being moved by a god who sits on a throne in the sky.

6) The Prophecies Are Faked. In Matthew 1:20–23 the author claims that Isaiah 7:14 predicts Jesus' virgin birth. The context for the prophecy in Isaiah tells us that before a son born of a "young woman" (not a virgin) "is old enough to know how to choose between right and wrong the countries of two kings (i.e., Syria and Samaria) will be destroyed" (7:15-16). The prophecy in the original Hebrew says nothing whatsoever about a virginal conception. Period. It says nothing about a messiah, either. The prophecy was actually fulfilled in Isaiah 8:3 with the birth of the son Maher-shalal-hash-baz.

The Hebrew word for virgin is *betulah*. It's used five times in the book of Isaiah. Isaiah 7:14 isn't one of them. The word used in Isaiah 7:14 is *almah*, which means young woman, or simply girl. It does not specify a virgin. Full Stop. The gospel of Matthew's error was to use a 200-year-old Greek translation of the Hebrew which used the word *parthenos*. Originally the Greek word *parthenos* meant "young girl," but by the time Matthew wrote his gospel that word had been changed by usage to signify a "virgin" rather than a young girl. This is not unlike how the words nice and gay have changed in meaning over the years. So Matthew grossly misunderstood the original Hebrew text in Isaiah by incorrectly claiming Jesus was to be born of a virgin.

A second prophecy in Isaiah 9:6–7 reads: "For to us a child is born, to us a son is given, and the government will be on his shoulders. And he will be called Wonderful Counselor, Mighty God, Everlasting Father, Prince of Peace." [See Luke 1:31-33] Any Jew writing at that time might express the same hope for a Messiah/savior who would rescue their nation from their oppressors. But an expressed hope for a future Messiah is not to be considered a prediction, unless along with that expressed hope are specific details whereby we can check to see if it was fulfilled in a specific person. Isaiah provides none. With no details, there isn't any real prediction.

German theologian Ute Ranke-Heinemann concludes after her own study: "If we wish to continue seeing Luke's accounts… as historical events, we'd have to take a large leap of faith: We'd have to assume that while on verifiable matters of historical fact Luke tells all sorts of fairy tales but on supernatural matters—which by definition can never be checked—he simply reports the facts. By his arbitrary treatment of history, Luke has shown himself to be an unhistorical reporter—a teller of fairy tales." [*Putting Away Childish Things*, p. 14]

7) The Virgin Birth of Jesus Has Pagan Parallels. Robert Miller shows us many important people in the ancient world were believed to have been the product of virgin births: "People in the ancient world believed that heroes were the sons of gods because of the extraordinary qualities of their adult lives, not because there was public information about the intimate details of how their mothers became pregnant. In fact, in some biographies, the god takes on the physical form of the woman's husband in order to have sex with her." [*Born Divine*, p. 134] And then he proceeds to document some of these stories. There was Theagenes, the Olympic champion, who was regarded as divine for being one of the greatest athletes in the ancient world. Hercules was the most widely revered hero of the ancient world. He was promoted to divine status after his death, and it was said he was fathered by Zeus. Alexander the Great was believed to be conceived of a virgin and fathered in turn by Heracles. Augustus Caesar was believed to be conceived of a virgin and fathered by Apollo, as was Plato, the

104

philosopher. Apollonius of Tyana was believed to be a holy man born of a virgin and fathered by Zeus. Pythagoras the philosopher was believed to be a son of Apollo. There were also savior-gods, like Krishna, Osiris, Dionysus, and Tammuz, who were born of virgins and known to the Gospel writers centuries before.

Justin Martyr was a second-century Christian apologist who tried to convince the pagans of his day of the truth of Christianity. In his First Apology to Roman people, he wrote:

> When we say that the Word, who is the first-birth of God, was produced without sexual union, and that he, Jesus Christ, our teacher, was crucified and died, and rose again, and ascended into heaven, we propound nothing different from what you believe regarding those whom you esteem sons of Jupiter...Of what kind of deeds recorded of each of these reputed sons of Jupiter, it is needless to tell to those who already know...[I]f we even affirm that he [Jesus] was born of a virgin, accept this in common with what you accept of Perseus.

All that these virgin birth claims show is that someone thought these people were important, and that's it. None of them is taken to be literal virgin births, probably not even in that day! So it should not come as a surprise that the early Christians came up with similar myths about Jesus. It's myth all the way down with no historical reality to it. There's no reason to accept this extraordinary claim at all.

Afterward, I wrote the following debate analysis.

An Analysis of My Recent Debate on the Virgin Birth of Jesus

I've already published my debate opener on the virgin birth. One of the best things about debates, for me anyway, is that they force me to write debate openers. They are succinct statements of why I don't believe. They will stand the test of time, even if public debates allow for the irrelevancies and non-sequiturs of my debate opponents to muddy the waters.

To write them means I must also participate in public debates, so I do. In this debate, I had some problems with the logistics for several reasons. It was supposed to give presenters 30 minutes each for their opening statements. That's was too long. So we agreed to limit it to 20 minutes just prior to the debate. I thought it would be better for the audience, and that I could fit my opener into that time. I was wrong. I was also wrong to ask my opponent to time it. There should've been someone chosen in the audience to time our debates, and to give us a 5-minute, 2 minutes, then 1-minute warning. There should also have been a moderator during our cross-examination, and someone to field questions for us during the Q & A period. I wasn't in charge of these details but I should have inquired. For without a moderator, we interrupted each other far too often. That's what happens without a moderator, and it sucked. Big Time! For I have a hard time listening and responding to utter nonsense.

I eventually got through my debate opener since, during the cross-examination phase, I finished it.

On the substantive issues, I did well.

One of the most significant points made by my opponent was based on an early Christian forgery called the *Proto-Gospel of James* (Dated 140-170 AD) which was falsely claimed to be written by James the brother of Jesus. This Gospel was rejected as authentic by the early church. It's supposed to provide the objective evidence that Jesus was born of a virgin named Mary, my opponent said. I didn't respond too well, but I did respond adequately. I had said such an account is irrelevant to the case for the virginity of Mary.

The Proto-Gospel of James follows a lot of what we read in the canonical gospel accounts, which is significant, since it repeats some of the fraudulent claims in the gospels, such as the world-wide census under Augustus Caesar, the sign of the Star, the slaughter of the innocents, and Bethlehem being the birthplace of Jesus, which my opening statement debunks. It also repeats the claim that Joseph was initially convinced by a dream that Mary was impregnated by God. *cough*

In the *Proto-Gospel of James* both Joseph and Mary participated in a barbaric trial by ordeal (based on passages like Numbers 5 quoted below). After drinking contaminated water, they did not show evidence of "sin," that is, adultery or fornication. Exonerated, right? No, not at all. Trial by ordeals do not work. They're barbaric and unbecoming of a God to require it. One might as well use it on people convicted of a capital crime to determine if juries were correct to find them guilty. If they pass the ordeal then free them, despite what juries had just determined. Why not? If the one in the Proto-Gospel of James is good, so is the other.

106

In the Proto-Gospel of James there was a midwife for Mary named Salome. She testified Mary was still a virgin after she gave birth to Jesus, and by doing so, provided testimony that Mary was also perpetual virgin! Reminiscent of the tale of Doubting Thomas, who refused to believe Jesus was resurrected until he saw Jesus and touched his wounds, Salome refused to believe Mary was a virgin until she checked Mary's hymen after the birth of Jesus! Upon testing Mary for an intact hymen her hand began to burn as if it caught on fire. Salome prays for forgiveness for questioning, and her hand was subsequently healed. [In the tale of Doubting Thomas, we're told to believe without seeing, whereas here we're told God is displeased when we question--even though in this case it supposedly produced a good result!]

A late dated forgery containing an additional miracle such as Salome's supposed healed hand doesn't provide support for the original miracle claim of the virgin birth. It isn't considered objective evidence nor is it considered good testimonial evidence. In fact, if it takes an additional miracle claim to support the original miracle claim of the virgin birth, then this compounds the problem of verification. That's because Salome's unevidenced miracle is not evidence for another unevidenced miracle of the virgin birth!

This forged gospel contains known historical falsehoods as it's based on what we read in the gospels. It is late, untrustworthy and inauthentic. It doesn't provide the needed objective evidence or testimonial evidence to support a miracle claim, as I mentioned in my opening statement. It is therefore irrelevant!

Trial by Ordeal, Numbers 5:16-27

16 'Then the priest shall bring her near and have her stand before the Lord, 17 and the priest shall take holy water in an earthenware vessel; and he shall take some of the dust that is on the floor of the tabernacle and put it into the water. 18 The priest shall then have the woman stand before the Lord and let the hair of the woman's head go loose, and place the grain offering of memorial in her hands, which is the grain offering of jealousy, and in the hand of the priest is to be the water of bitterness that brings a curse. 19 The priest shall have her take an oath and shall say to the woman, "If no man

has lain with you and if you have not gone astray into uncleanness, being under the authority of your husband, be immune to this water of bitterness that brings a curse; 20 if you, however, have gone astray, being under the authority of your husband, and if you have defiled yourself and a man other than your husband has had intercourse with you" 21 (then the priest shall have the woman swear with the oath of the curse, and the priest shall say to the woman), "the Lord make you a curse and an oath among your people by the Lord's making your thigh waste away and your abdomen swell; 22 and this water that brings a curse shall go into your stomach, and make your abdomen swell and your thigh waste away." And the woman shall say, "Amen. Amen."

23 'The priest shall then write these curses on a scroll, and he shall wash them off into the water of bitterness. 24 Then he shall make the woman drink the water of bitterness that brings a curse, so that the water which brings a curse will go into her and cause bitterness. 25 The priest shall take the grain offering of jealousy from the woman's hand, and he shall wave the grain offering before the Lord and bring it to the altar; 26 and the priest shall take a handful of the grain offering as its memorial offering and offer it up in smoke on the altar, and afterward he shall make the woman drink the water. 27 When he has made her drink the water, then it shall come about, if she has defiled herself and has been unfaithful to her husband, that the water which brings a curse will go into her and cause bitterness, and her abdomen will swell and her thigh will waste away, and the woman will become a curse among her people. 28 But if the woman has not defiled herself and is clean, she will then be free and conceive children.

11 - Did Jesus Rise from the Dead? Loftus vs Abdu Murray

I'm very honored to be here and happy people actually showed up to listen to this debate. I have a lot of ground to cover so I must begin.

Most of what I'll be saying can be found in two books of mine, *Why I Became an Atheist,* is my magnum opus, and *How to Defend the Christian* Faith: *Advice from an Atheist.* If you disagree with anything I say, then I refer you to them for more.

Tonight, I'll start with the current state of Christian apologetics, and then I'll deal with the so-called evidence for the resurrection of Jesus. Finally, I'll pull it all together in the end.

Christian Apologetics:

I'll start with a quote from Cardinal Avery Dulles: "The 20th century has seen more clearly than previous periods that apologetics stands or falls with the question of method."[1] I'm going to highlight this tonight, something most apologists haven't quite considered before.

On Apologetics and Method, Definitions and Argument

Apologetics = Defending the truth of Christianity.

Method = Developing the most effective strategy defending Christianity.

My contention is that all apologetics is special pleading! Everything said in defense of Christianity operates by an unreasonable double standard. Apologists treat Christianity differently than they treat the evidences of all the other religions they reject.

---

[1] Dulles, Avery (1971), *A History of Apologetics*, New York: Corpus Books, p. 246.

Case in point: One should first come up with the best method to know which religion is true, if there is one, rather than coming up with a method that can be used to defend one's religion, after believing in a religion. This problem has only recently come to light, and it's significant. In response, apologists are trying to come up with a method, after the fact, that justifies their faith. Folks, this is not how it's honestly done! Method must come first.

Christian Apologetics Is in Serious Crisis!

In 1953, Bernard Ramm brought attention to this problem in his book *Varieties of Christian Apologetics*, which were discussed and debated in subsequent books on the subject:

1976 Gordon Lewis, *Testing Christianity's Truth Claims: Approaches to Christian Apologetics.*

2000 Steven B. Cowan, ed., *Five Views of Apologetics.*

2006 Kenneth Boa and Robert Bowman *Faith Has Its Reasons.*

From this fractured landscape, we can discern that apologist appear to use at least six different methods:

1)   Evidential Method

This is the only reasonable method for assessing the truth of religious faiths. It requires sufficient objective evidence to believe. The kicker is that so do most Christian apologists who reject it in favor of the other methods. The reason is because they know their faith doesn't meet this requirement.

Evidential Method: An Admitted Failure

a) Without God, Miracles Aren't Likely. The reason is stated adequately by apologist Norman Geisler: "Historical evidence alone is insufficient to believe Jesus arose from the dead and that God exists." He goes on to say, "The mere fact of the resurrection [of Jesus] cannot be used to establish the truth that there is a God. For the resurrection cannot even be a miracle unless there already is a God."[1]

b) Lessing's Ugly Broad Ditch. 18th-century German critic Gotthold Lessing wrote:

> "Miracles, which I see with my own eyes, and which I have opportunity to verify for myself, are one thing; miracles, of which I know only from history that others say they have seen them and verified them, are another."[2]

Bart Ehrman echoes Lessing:

> "All that historians can do is show what probably happened in the past. That is the problem inherent in miracles. Miracles, by our very definition of the term, are virtually impossible events," so "miracles, by their very nature, are always the least probable explanations for what happened."[3]

Deists were the first modern evidentialists (which peaked 1696 – 1801). Deism began as a method for gaining religious truth. It was based on sufficient evidence, but it ended with the rejection of all religious dogmas except for the need of a creator. After Darwin's *Origin of Species,* most deists became atheists. That's because the evidence leads there!

2) Classical Method

So to correct for the failures of evidentialism, apologists adopted a 2-step method, summed up as follows:

i) First argue to the existence of a god;
ii) Then to the resurrection.

---

[1] Geisler, Norman (1988), *Christian Apologetics,* Ada, MI: Baker Publishing Group, p. 95.
[2] "On the Proof of the Spirit and of Power," in *Lessing's Theological Writings,* trs, Henry Chadwick (1956), Stanford, CA: Stanford University Press, pp. 51-55.
[3] Ehrman, Bart (2009), *Jesus Interrupted,* New York: Harper Collins, p. 174.

But do theistic arguments work? Two of the greatest living Christian apologists are Alvin Plantinga and Richard Swinburne. Plantinga has admitted theistic arguments don't work, saying, "I don't know of an argument for Christian belief that seems very likely to convince one who doesn't already accept its conclusion...if Christian beliefs are true, then the most satisfactory way to hold them will not be as the conclusions of argument."[1] Swinburne specifically rejects the Moral Argument to God's existence, saying, "I cannot see any force in an argument to the existence of God from the existence of morality."[2] Another Christian apologist of note is John Feinberg. He wrote, "I am not convinced that any of the traditional arguments [for God's existence] succeeds."[3] Now if they don't think these arguments work why should any of us? It's not just me who is saying this. It's what Christian apologists themselves say.

Even if so, which god? Deist god? Allah? A non-personal force? An evil god? A scientific god who is watching us like rats in a maze?

It only grants miracles are possible. If there is a creator god, miracles are possible! But I grant miracles are possible even as an atheist! There's nothing all that controversial about this.

It ends up being nothing more than a dressed up evidentialism! For believing in a creator god does not tell us which god exists. One must still look at the evidence just as I do. So the classical method brings apologists back where they started from, forced to deal with the evidence, which is something they had hoped to avoid.

3) Presuppositional "Method"

Summed up: "The evidence for the resurrection can only be accepted through the lens of Christian assumptions."

---

[1] Plantinga, Alvin (2000), *Warranted Christian Belief*, Oxford: Oxford University Press, p. 201.
[2] Swinburne, Richard (2004), *The Existence of God*, Oxford: Oxford University Press, p. 215.
[3] Feinberg, John S. (2013), *Can You Believe It's True: Christian Apologetics in a Modern & Postmodern Era*, Wheaton, IL: Crossway, p. 321.

But where do these assumptions come from? How is it possible to start with assumptions without first looking at the evidence? The evidence must come first. That makes the assumptions carry all of the weight as evidence. Consistency means allowing Muslim assumptions as their evidence, or Mormon assumptions as their evidence. This non-method tacitly admits there isn't sufficient evidence to believe in the resurrection. Otherwise, it would never have been concocted.

This "begs the question." Other Christian apologists agree. It's not just me saying this.

4) Reformed "Method"

Summed up: "It's reasonable to believe in God and the resurrection without the need for and/or the existence of sufficient objective evidence."

Who would ever say such a thing? This is another admission by apologists themselves, that there isn't sufficient objective evidence to believe. For if it existed then this non-method would never have been concocted.

This requires psychic ability, since it's argued the spirit world communicates to believers what happened three days after Jesus was crucified. How else can we reasonably know what happened in history except by using the historical method?

5) Fideism "Method"

Summed up: "Private subjective experiences (PSE) of a risen Jesus provide good reasons to believe."

But PSE are only evidence of PSE. They are only evidence of private subjective states of the mind. They say nothing about the objective world.

This is the method of insanity! Folks, this may sound offensive but this is the method of insane people in psyche wards, who think they are Jesus!

113

It's unreliable as a historical method. It's not a method at all! Can anyone use this method to know what happened at Custer's Last Stand? It too concedes Christianity does not have sufficient objective evidence for it. Christian apologists admit this. It's not just me saying it.

6) Cumulative "Method"

Summed up: "The apologist needs to be able to employ different approaches in different contexts. Every person will react and be reached differently, so there is *no* one *approach that will work every time.*" –Wayne House & Dennis Jowers.[1]

Who would ever say such a thing? Apologists are searching for a method that works to convince others, rather than one that helps us arrive at the truth. That's the context of what they wrote. Its exhibit A in revealing the truth about apologetics. The goal is to persuade. The method is special pleading. Whatever works is what they'll adopt. It is the warp and woof of Christian apologetics.

This method is like mixing oil and water. I fail to see how evidentialism, the Classical method, presuppositionalism and fideism can be harmonized or reconciled.

Leaky bucket problem. Since all methods have gaping holes in them, putting them together doesn't stop the leaks.

Proponents merely agree on the conclusion, that's it! What we see here are Christians struggling to develop a method that supports their prior faith, rather than developing an objective method that leads to the truth about religions. As you can see, they struggle precisely because they reject evidentialism.

The Results on Method:

We can see from the previous summaries that the Christian (apologist) is left in an unsatisfactory position.

---

[1] This sentence occurs at the end of chapter 3 on "Approaches to Apologetics," where they had just discussed the apologetic methods I did. House, Wayne & Jowers, Dennis (2011), *Reasons for Our Hope: An Introduction to Christian Apologetics*, Nashville, B&H Academic, p. 47.

- Evidentialist: It's an admitted failure in defending Christianity! Evidentialism led to deism and to atheism.
- Classical Method: Back to Evidentialism! A god belief doesn't change anything.
- Presuppositionalism Method: Question begging!
- Reformed Method: Psychic ability! Completely by-passes historical inquiry.
- Fideism "Method": The method of Insanity! Unreliable as a historical method.
- Cumulative Method: Faith in search of a method! This is what's really going on!

The Kicker:

Since there are six major methods, then any given one of them is rejected by 83% of apologists! i.e., 83% of apologists reject the need for and/or existence of sufficient objective evidence.

What if Mormons admitted that?

Outsider Test for Faith Method

Summed up: "This is the only way to get believers to see the value of the evidential method. It asks believers to test their own religious faith from the perspective of an outsider by applying the same consistent level of reasonable skepticism to them all." I've defended this in my book, *The Outsider Test for Faith.*

Now for the evidence of the resurrection of Jesus:

Assume you have never heard about Christianity. Abdu is a missionary from China preaching Yingianity, a newly discovered religion.

Why Do This?

It's the only way to evaluate one's culturally inherited religious faith because we seek to confirm rather than disconfirm our beliefs!

Because we depend on familiarity. Here's an example: If you're a Christian you see nothing bizarre about the gospel story involving one member of a Trinitarian god who came down to earth by being born of a virgin, who was 100% god and yet 100% man, to be killed so the other two members of the trinity could forgive people who believed that story, and then was raised from dead and ascended into the sky to return to the Trinitarian throne, bringing back to reign with him the sinless man Jesus, who is forever joined to him at the hip.

Because we depend on our cultures. We are products of our times and indoctrinated into our cultures. Culture isn't even something we see until we focus on it. For cultures allow us to see in the first place. Cultures are the very lens through which we view the world. And this is a Christian culture we live in, especially if you were raised to believe.

Because our brains lie to us! Cognitive biases get in the way of evaluating your own religious faith. The mother of all cognitive biases is confirmation bias, which is the strong tendency to search for data and/or interpret existing data in ways that confirm one's prior beliefs. This bias forces believers to misjudge the probabilities in favor of their faith. The brain only cares if what it concludes helps it to survive. The brain evolved to act this way for self-preservation purposes. It maintains and defends its beliefs so you can survive as a social creature, since you need others to survive! You will defend the beliefs of your social group in order to stay within the safety net of your social group, irrespective of whether those beliefs are true or not. There is a massive amount or solid research supportive of these undeniable facts.

What Would it Take to Accept Abdu's Yingianity?

It would take an overwhelming amount of strong historical evidence to overcome our concrete personal experience that dead men stay dead.

Where's the Empirical Evidence?

There is none!
Because it supposedly happened in the ancient pre-scientific past, in a lone part of the planet, before investigative reporters, videos and cell phones!

Where's The Textual Evidence?

There is none!
i.e.: No original texts!
We must wait until the 4th century to get full manuscripts
Contains forgeries. Pastoral Letters. Ending of Mark. II Peter. Bart Ehrman's works have proven this.
Excludes other Christian writings. Judaizers. Gnostics. See Bart Ehrman's books, *Lost Scriptures* and *Lost Christianities*.

Where's The First Hand Testimonial Evidence?

There is none!
There were no eyewitnesses to the resurrection. No one can say "I saw Jesus as he was raised from the dead." No eyewitnesses wrote anything either. We do not have anything written directly by Jesus himself or any of his original disciples.
All supposed testimonies to the resurrection of Jesus are reported to us by others, which is considered inadmissible in court because it's hearsay evidence. Subsequent gospel writers plagiarized from Mark, the first gospel. So the gospel stories of Jesus' resurrection stand on Mark's gospel

117

alone, and at the end of his gospel there isn't a sequence where Jesus shows himself alive after dying.

We don't have a chance to question anyone. There is a reason why hearsay testimony is not allowed in our courtrooms. How do we really know what they actually testified to? Did they actually see the risen Jesus as claimed? Did they all tell the same story? Did any of them recant later? Just think of Mormon origins.

Comes from admitted visionaries. Paul is the only writer to claim he had seen the risen Jesus and his letters are the earliest testimony we have of it. But we have serious difficulties in knowing what he saw. On the Damascus Road he never claimed to have actually seen or touched Jesus (see Galatians 1; Acts 9; 22; 26). He specifically said it was a visionary experience (Acts 26:19; see 9:17), and that he had many of them (2 Corinthians 12:1-7; see 1 Corinthians 9:1, Acts 16:9-10; 18:9; 22:17-18; 23:11, Galatians 2:2). Paul repeatedly speaks of "revelations" which he passed down to the church (1 Cor. 2:13; 7:40; 14:37). He even says he learned about the "Lord's Supper" from "the Lord" himself (1 Corinthians 11:23). Paul even claimed he got his whole gospel from a private revelation (Galatians 1:11-12). Paul's early churches were visionaries too (Acts 2:17), where "young men saw visions." They were convinced they were receiving divine messages from Jesus and expressed them through the "spiritual gifts" of divine "wisdom," "knowledge," "prophecy" or "tongues" (2 Corinthians 12:7-10). The writer of the book of Revelation (2-3) said he received seven letters to the seven churches in a private revelation.

Paul equates his own visionary experience of the risen Jesus with the witnesses he mentioned in I Corinthians 15:3-8, so their testimony cannot be considered any better than Paul's.

These are all private subjective experiences. Why should we accept that these private revelations came from God? I see no reason why we should.

Where's the Prophetic Evidence?

There is none! I defy someone to come up with one statement in the Old Testament that is specifically fulfilled in the life, death, and resurrection of Jesus that can legitimately be understood as a prophecy and singularly points to Jesus as the Messiah using today's historical-grammatical herme-neutical method. It cannot be done. An expressed hope for a future savior is not to be considered a prediction, unless along with that hope are specific details whereby we can check to see if it was fulfilled in a specific person.

No prophecy of a Trinitarian God. OT Texts like "Let us make man in our image" are describing polytheism.

No prophecy of an Incarnation or Virgin birth. In Matthew 1:20–23 the author claims that Isaiah 7:14 refers to Jesus' virgin birth calling him "Immanuel (of God) with us." The context for the prophecy in Isaiah tells us that before any "young woman" (not virgin) shall conceive and bear a son who grows to maturity the southern Israelite kingdom of Ahaz, would be devastated. The prophecy says nothing whatsoever about a virginal concep-tion. And it says nothing about a Messiah, either. The prophecy was actually fulfilled in Isaiah 8:3 with the birth of the child king Maher-shalalhash-baz. All kings we're thought of as divine anyway.

No prophecy of a dying Messiah. The Suffering Servant in Isaiah was Israel. 49:3: God says, "You are my servant, Israel, in whom I will dis-play my splendor." The Psalms were not predicting anything about the death of Jesus either. They are merely prayers in times of affliction that the NT writers applied to Jesus out of context.

No prophecy of a resurrection. It doesn't exist in the OT.

Where's the Corroborative Evidence?

There is none!

Nothing from any contemporaries. We don't have anything written by the Jewish leaders or by the Romans that mentions Jesus, the content of his preaching, why he was killed, or what they thought about claims that he had been resurrected. Wouldn't you want to know what they said if you were really interested in knowing the truth? So given that we don't know what they thought isn't the intellectually honest thing to do is to admit you don't know after all?

Bizarre unbelievable stories of zombies, earthquakes and eclipses. We have no independent reports that the veil of the temple was torn in two at Jesus' death (Mark 15:38), nor that darkness came "over the whole land" from noon until three in the afternoon (Mark 15:33), nor that "the sun stopped shining" (Luke 23:45), nor that there was an earthquake at his death (Matt. 27:51, 54), with another "violent" one the day he arose from the grave (Matt. 28:2), nor that the saints were raised to life at his death and at his resurrection "went into the holy city and appeared to many people" and were never heard from again (Matt. 27:52–53). Could these events really have occurred without subsequent Roman or rabbinic literature mentioning them? These silences are telling.

The Results

The results are in and it doesn't look good for the Christian, since there is...
- No empirical evidence
- No original texts
- No first-hand testimonial evidence
- No prophetic evidence
- No corroborative evidence

Case in Point: The Jews and The Evidence:

The Jews were...
- Beloved of God
- Believed in God
- Believed God does miracles
- Hoped for a Messiah
- Knew their prophecies

But overwhelming numbers of them did not believe!

Since these Jews were there and didn't believe, why should we? No, really. Why should we? Why should anyone? The usual answer is that these Jews didn't want to believe because Jesus was not their kind of Messiah, a king who would throw off Roman rule. But then, where did they get that idea in the first place? They got it from their own scriptures. And who supposedly penned them? Their God.

I am baffled as to why an omniscient God could not think of any other way to have Jesus crucified but by using the Jews to instigate it. But because he couldn't, God needed to mislead the Jews about the nature of their Messiah. So due to this loving plan of his, Christians have been given a reason to persecute and kill Jews for centuries for being Christ killers [the Romans are actually the guilty ones]. Not only this, but the overwhelming majority of Jews will go to hell where Judas is waiting for them. *If anyone was sacrificed for the sins of the world it would be Judas and the Jews.* Does this sound fair for a perfectly good, omniscient judge?

Think like an outsider for the first time in your lives!

Consider this 800-page book by Michael Alter, *The Resurrection: A Critical Inquiry.* It's the best book of its kind, an encyclopedic refutation of the resurrection of Jesus hypothesis. The stunning fact is that it's not written by an atheist. It's written by a believer, a theist, just not Abdu's kind of theist. He's a Jew.

So What It Would Take to Accept Abdu's Yingianity?

It would take an overwhelming amount of strong historical evidence to overcome our concrete personal experience that dead men stay dead. Let this sink in before proceeding.

Decision Time:

Would you accept Yingianity given this non-evidence, if 83% of Ying apologists rejected the need for and/or existence of sufficient objective evidence?

You would not accept Yingianity!
You should not accept Christianity!

PART 2: A DEEPER INCURSION

In this section, I wanted to include some previously unreleased material that can help lead the charge as a continuation from Part 1. I will tackle a few select topics in greater depth.

12 – The Argument from the Scale of the Universe

Here, I'll attempt to defend Nicholas Everitt's argument from the scale of the universe. His arguments can be found on pages 215-226 in his book *The Non-Existence of God*,[1] which I will be quoting from.

When we talk about the scale of the universe, we mean both its vastness and its age. When I look at pictures of the universe, I conclude that we human beings live on a mere small pale blue dot[2] that will last a short while and then cease to exist. For nonbelievers like me, there is strong intuitive appeal that this universe is not what we would expect if theism is true.

Nicholas Everitt makes an argument based on these facts from the scale of the universe. He puts the question this way: "Is the universe as it is revealed to us by modern science roughly the sort of universe which we would antecedently expect a God of traditional theism to create? The short answer to this is 'No'. In almost every respect, the universe as it is revealed to us by modern science is hugely unlike the sort of universe which the traditional thesis would lead us to expect."[3] "The evidence," he says, "by itself

---

[1] Everitt, Nicholas (2004), *The Non-Existence of God*, London: Routledge.
[2] A phrase derived from the "Pale Blue Dot" photograph of planet Earth taken on February 14, 1990, by the *Voyager 1* space probe from a record distance of about 3.7 billion miles away. The planet, from there, looks like a blueish-white speck.
[3] Ibid, p. 216.

is not very strong, certainly not overwhelming, but it is nonetheless significant."[1]

Everitt writes:[2]

> Traditional theism would lead you to expect human beings to ap-
> pear fairly soon after the start of the universe. For, given the central role
> of humanity, what would be the point of a universe which came into ex-
> istence and then existed for unimaginable aeons without the presence
> of the very species that supplied its rationale? You would expect hu-
> mans to appear after a great many animals, since the animals are
> subordinate species available for human utilization, and there would be
> no point in having humans arrive on the scene needing animals (e.g. as
> a source of food, or clothing, or companionship) only for them to dis-
> cover that animals had not yet been created. But equally, you would not
> expect humans to arrive very long after the animals, for what would be
> the point of a universe existing for aeons full of animals created for hu-
> manity's delectation, in the absence of any humans? Further, you would
> expect the earth to be fairly near the centre of the universe if it had one,
> or at some similarly significant location if it did not have an actual centre.
> You would expect the total universe to be not many orders of magni-
> tude greater than the size of the earth. The universe would be on a
> human scale. You would expect that even if there are regions of the cre-
> ated world which are hostile to human life, and which perhaps are
> incompatible with it, the greater part of the universe would be accessi-
> ble to human exploration. If this were not so, what would the point be
> of God creating it?
>
> These expectations are largely what we find in the Genesis story
> (or strictly, stories) of creation. There is, then, a logic to the picture of
> the universe with which the Genesis story presents us: given the initial
> assumptions about God, his nature, and his intentions, the Genesis uni-
> verse is pretty much how it would be reasonable for God to proceed.
> Given the hypothesis of theism and no scientific knowledge, and then
> asked to construct a picture of the universe and its creation, it is not sur-
> prising that the author(s) of Genesis came up with the account which
> they did.

Everitt argues that this universe is not what we would expect to find
prior to our discovery of the scale of the universe given the supposition of
classical theism, where "God decides to create a universe in which human

---

[1] Ibid, p.213.
[2] Ibid, pp. 215-216.

beings will be the jewel" of his creation, and of whom "God will have an especial care for human beings."[1]

He puts his argument into this form:[2]

> (1) If the God of classical theism existed, with the purposes traditionally ascribed to him, then he would create a universe on a human scale, i.e. one that is not unimaginably large, unimaginably old, and in which human beings form an unimaginably tiny part of it, temporally and spatially.
>
> (2) The world does not display a human scale. So,
>
> (3) There is evidence against the hypothesis that the God of classical theism exists with the purposes traditionally ascribed to him.

He admits the limited nature of this conclusion when he says, "it is not a proof of the falsity of theism. We can also add that as presented, it does not even claim that theism is probably false," although, "the argument is not negligible.... The findings of modern science tell against the truth of theism."[3] "There is indeed a mismatch between the universe as revealed to us by modern science and the universe which we would expect, given the hypothesis of theism."[4]

The crucial premise seems to be the first one. A key supposition is that "human beings will be the jewel" of God's creation, and of whom "God will have an especial care for human beings."[5] It's based upon what we would expect from such a God given the purposes traditionally ascribed to him.

He's asking us what we would expect to find before we had any scientific knowledge about the universe, given the fact that mankind is the pinnacle of creation in that universe. It concerns what one would predict based upon what one believes, since being able to accurately predict something confirms what one believes (whereas not being able to do so, is disconfirming evidence). As far as what one should expect given the existence of some x, there is a big difference between (1) finding what we expect to find given x, and (2) finding something different than what we expect to

---

[1] Ibid, p. 215.
[2] Ibid, p. 225.
[3] Ibid, p. 216.
[4] Ibid, p. 225.
[5] Ibid, p. 215.

find given x. When one thinks about this, it becomes obvious that (1) is to be considered evidence on behalf of x, whereas (2) is to be considered counter-evidence against x. This argument is similar to Rawl's "veil of ignorance." What would you expect to find give theistic assumptions about God's purposes before actually experiencing the world?

Everitt illustrates what he's doing with a figure like Robinson Crusoe, who wonders whether or not, after the shipwreck, there is another survivor on the island. Given such a hypothesis, Crusoe should be able to make some predictions about what that other survivor would do, such that, if he did, then Crusoe would see signs that he did (like marks on the trees, whistling, singing, having fires at night, and so forth). Things that confirm his expectations constitute evidence that there is another survivor. Things that don't confirm his expectations constitute evidence against there being another survivor.

What Everitt is Not Arguing For

Let me start by explaining what Everitt is *not* arguing for. In chapter 5 from Richard Purtill's 1974 book, *Reason to Believe*,[1] Purtill argues with an entirely different argument when he wrote:

> Christianity arose when the universe seemed a smaller and cozier affair. Now that science has shown us the true age and size of the universe, we can no longer accept the idea of a God who is personally concerned with our conduct or our consciences. If any creative power is the cause of the physical universe it has no interest in us. The idea of God explains nothing and changes nothing. For modern man, God is dead.

Purtill continues:

> Now this is hardly worthy of the name of argument. From 'the universe is very large and old' it does not follow that 'God takes no interest in man' unless we add further premises. And as we will see, these further premises have no plausibility at all. But the emotional force of the size

---

[1] Found online at https://www.google.com/books/edition/Reason_to_Believe/5YtHDwAAQBAJ?hl=en&gbpv=1 (Accessed 26/05/2022).

and age of the universe, once it is imaginatively grasped, is very great. To many people the universe, as science shows it to us, does not feel like the sort of universe which would be made by a personal god. And since many people think mainly with their emotions, there seems to them to be an argument.

This isn't what Everitt is arguing for. Purtill is discussing an emotional argument where it seems as though God couldn't be that interested in us if he created such a vast universe. He answers this difficulty by saying that since God is infinite, he can indeed pay attention to human beings on a tiny pale blue dot called earth. And while I think this particular difficulty does indeed have a great deal of emotional force to it from my perspective, I'd have to agree with Purtill that it is a purely emotional one and, as such, is probably not an argument that would convince believers. Everitt's argument is not an emotional one. It does not suffer the same fate as what Purtill argues against.

That being said, I do not believe human beings are logical machines. We are influenced to believe what we do by our social backgrounds, peer pressure groups, dreams, aspirations and emotions. And, as such, there can be no complete separation from what one feels and what one thinks. There will always be a component of emotion included in our logical evaluations of these matters, and vice versa. I know people, smart people, who can logically defend something that they believe entirely for emotional reasons. How else can those of us who disagree with the Mormons or the Muslims explain what they believe any other way? And for this same reason the emotional force of the problem of evil or suffering is not one to be taken lightly either.

Again, Everitt argues that this universe is not what we would expect to find given the supposition of the classical God of Christianity, where "God decides to create a universe in which human beings will be the jewel" of his creation, and of whom "God will have an especial care for human beings."[1]

Everitt's argument is also not about whether certain present-day beliefs about theism are essential to theism. Peter van Inwagen wrote:[2]

---

[1] Everitt (2004), p. 215.
[2] Peter van Inwagen, "Reply to Sean Carroll," *Faith and Philosophy*, vol. 22, 5, 2005, p. 637.

A lot of what theists believed about the *mundus* [the physical universe] and its contents has turned out to be wrong: that the earth is at its center, for example, that God had created it in essentially its present form about four thousand years before the birth of Christ, that a living organism can exist only if a rational agent has imposed the form definitive of its species on a particular parcel of matter .... But none of these theses was essential to theism, and theists, a few radical and intellectually marginalized Protestants apart, gave them up with less fuss than atheists have generally displayed in giving up the idea of a physical universe that has an eternal, uniform past.

Van Inwagen's point can be granted. For there is indeed nothing on hindsight that is essential to theism and which demands a smaller, human-scaled universe. In one sense what theists consider essential to theism has changed and is continually changing, anyway, with the advancement of science. In any case, the issue concerns what theists would have expected (and did in fact expect) prior to the advancement of modern science with the discovery of the large scaled universe we all live in.

The Argument Confirms My Expectations

There is just something about Everitt's argument that resonates with me. It confirms my expectations, and as such confirms for me that God doesn't exist. I think the argument is a good one even if theists and skeptics themselves might disagree with me. It's no reason to cease making a particular argument merely because people disagree with you on both sides of the fence. In my view, most arguments between us serve only to confirm what we each separately believe anyway. I don't even see a reason why my intellectual opponents must agree that an argument is a sound one before it can be said to be a good one. Remember, a sound argument is deductively valid with true premises. So until we can all agree what makes an argument a good one, don't say this is not a good one without good criteria for doing so.

Atheist scholar Richard Carrier apparently agreed with Everitt and me on this when he wrote the following:[1]

---

[1] "Why I Am Not a Christian," found at http://www.infidels.org/library, section 4, "Christianity Predicts a Different Universe".

For the Christian theory does not predict what we observe, while the natural theory does predict what we observe. After all, what need does an intelligent engineer have of billions of years and trillions of galaxies filled with billions of stars each? That tremendous waste is only needed if life had to arise by natural accident. It would have no plausible purpose in the Christian God's plan. You cannot predict from "the Christian God created the world" that "the world" would be trillions of galaxies large and billions of years old before it finally stumbled on one rare occasion of life. But we can predict exactly that from "no God created this world." Therefore, the facts confirm atheism rather than theism. Obviously, a Christian can invent all manner of additional "ad hoc" theories to explain "why" his God would go to all the trouble of designing the universe to look exactly like we would expect it to look if God did not exist. But these "ad hoc" excuses are themselves pure concoctions of the imagination--until the Christian can prove these additional theories are true, from independent evidence, there is no reason to believe them, and hence no reason to believe the Christian theory.

I think Everitt's argument is sound, and convincing, but as he admits, it does not show theism is "probably false." That being said, I think a stronger version of his argument can be made against evangelical Christianity, which believes the Bible is God's Word, regardless of whether or not the adherents are young earth creationists. That said, given the age of the universe at 13.5 billion years, it probably applies more to evangelicals who believe the universe is that old.

It's to evangelical Christianity I will henceforth argue my case, and as such, the rest that follows should be considered my own argument, not Everitt's, although I use his argument as a basis for mine. I will attempt to draw the conclusion that evangelical Christianity is probably false from what follows.

There is no understandable reason why God had to create such a large universe on such a scale if the drama on Earth is the most important game in town. If God wanted a cosmic showdown with the Devil, then all he needed to create was a flat disk, or a huge room, or the earth alone, without any stars. There would be no understandable reason for creating anything else, if the struggle for human hearts was the main (and probably the only) reason for creating in the first place, which is what I'm told. It doesn't make sense. It's not what one would expect, even being cautious with what we'd expect.

129

This argument depends to some degree on whether or not God might have other purposes for creating such a universe even granting mankind as the jewel of his creation, and whether or not, given the existence of an infinitely creative mind, he would have made the universe on such a scale as we find it. I will deal with these objections later.

Biblical Support

Let me offer some Biblical support for the claim that human beings are the apex of God's creation. The Bible strongly indicates that humans are so valuable to God that he created it all just for us. Then God visited us, died for our sins, and accepts the saints into heaven and casts sinners into hell.

Figure 1: James L. Christian, Philosophy: An Introduction to the Art of Wondering, 6th ed.,(Harcourt, 1994), p. 512.

The Bible led believers to think they lived in the center of the universe, which was small in scope. Just take a look at what the Bible says about the universe. Read this with a pre-scientific viewpoint, not with an *ex post facto* post-scientific reader's viewpoint, and it is clear what they seem to have believed. See diagram, below. This is especially so when we consider that the creation account in Genesis 1 starts first with the Earth being formed out of the chaotic waters (not created *ex nihilo*—out of nothing). Later (on the 4th day) the universe of stars is created to surround it. As mentioned, it is very probable that pre-scientific ancient people thought this way about the universe:

It doesn't take much theology to see that mankind is the apex, or the most important reason for creation. Take the following conclusions from scholars:

> The biblical view starts with the assertion that the eternal God has created man, the most significant of all his created works." "Man is not only God's creation, but the pinnacle of his creative effort...man is distinct, the high point of God's creative work, the apex of his handicraft. The progression of the created things in Genesis 1 is climatic; all of God's created work culminated in his fashioning of man. - Ronald B. Allen in "Man, Doctrine of," *Baker Encyclopedia of the Bible.*

> Having first called the earth into existence with its various requisites for human life, God then declared for the making of man. The impression that the Genesis account gives is that man was the special focus of God's creative purpose. It is not so much that man was the crown of God's creative acts, or the climax of the process, for although last in the ascending scale, he is first in the divine intention. All the previous acts of God are presented more in the nature of a continuous series...Then God said, 'Let us make man.' Then--when? When the cosmic order was finished, when the earth was ready to sustain man. Thus while man stands before God in a relationship of created dependence, he has also the status of a unique and special personhood in relation to God. - H. D. McDonald in "Man, Doctrine of.," *Evangelical Dictionary of Theology.*

> Man reflects God in a unique manner. Man is thus different from other forms of created organic life, over which he has been given dominion...he reflects the Creator in a way unparalleled by anything else in creation. - R.K. Harrison, "Old Testament Theology," *Evangelical Dictionary of Theology.*

> Genesis 1:26-30 shows human beings as the crown of creation...the image of God...probably means that God makes beings with whom he can communicate and who can respond, because, in contrast to the rest of nature, they are like him. So humanity receives the divine blessing and is given the role of God's vice-regent...to have dominion or control over the future course of the world. - J.R. Porter "Creation," *The Oxford Companion to the Bible.*

> The Genesis account of creation accords to man a supreme place in the cosmos. - "Man," *New Bible Dictionary.*

> ...the creation of humanity is surely accented as the climactic achievement of God's creative activity. - *The Anchor Bible Dictionary* (1:1166)

The reason I pulled these quotes out of dictionaries and encyclopedias, both conservative and liberal, is because they usually express the prevailing consensus on such matters, and each one of them was written by a scholar in their own right who had published articles and books on this topic.

According to these scholars, the creating of human beings is the culmination of creation itself, the crown of creation, the apex of creation, and as vice-regents over it they are surely to be considered the reason for creation itself, if not the most important reason for creation.

And the scholars do so for good reason. Isaiah 45:18 says: "For this is what the Lord says—he who created the heavens, he is God; he who fashioned and made the earth, he founded it; he did not create it to be empty, but formed it to be inhabited."

That is, the purpose of creation ("heavens" and "earth") was that it should be inhabited. Coupled with the fact that in Genesis God tells human beings that they are the rulers of his creation and are made in his image, that they are the purpose for God creating it in the first place.

The testing of our souls and redemption itself confirms this viewpoint. In the case of Job, the testing of his soul had significance for the unseen heavenly world, or at least, so say evangelical commentators. God even visited Earth in his Son to redeem not only sinful humanity, who caused this whole mess (as provoked by Satan), but creation itself, or so say conservative exegetes.

Paul's interpretation of the fall also supports this view, for he says it adversely affected all creation (Romans 8:19-23):

> The creation waits in eager expectation for the sons of God to be revealed. For the creation was subjected to frustration, not by its own choice, but by the will of the one who subjected it, in hope that the creation itself will be liberated from its bondage to decay and brought into the glorious freedom of the children of God. We know that the whole creation has been groaning as in the pains of childbirth right up to the present time. Not only so, but we ourselves, who have the firstfruits of

the Spirit, groan inwardly as we wait eagerly for our adoption as sons, the redemption of our bodies.

Paul said all of creation (i.e., the universe itself and all creatures living in and depending on that universe) was adversely affected by Adam and Eve's sin, so that means if Paul is correct, and if there are aliens, then they were also adversely affected by what Adam and Eve did. This would strongly suggest that aliens are also under our rule and that their status before God is below ours. Paul also wrote that Christ is reconciling all things unto himself "whether they be things in earth, or things in heaven" (Col 1:20).

I think Paul's theology of the fall and of reconciliation demand that what happens on Earth through human beings (as the apex of God's creative handiwork and through the God-man Jesus) affects all of creation, which includes the whole universe, according to the Bible.

In the Gospel of Matthew (16:19), we also learn that what the apostles bind and loose on Earth will be bound and loosed in heaven, and that could only mean the church is God's set of ruling representatives in the universe as a whole.

If passages such as these do not indicate that what happens on Earth by humans is the most important game in all of creation, or that Christians who believed the Bible before the rise of modern astronomy should have known better than to believe what this implies, then I simply am at a loss for words. The word "delusionary" comes to mind.

Consider also that when it comes to the problem of evil and the free will God supposedly granted to human beings, it's typically argued by Christians that God wanted free-willed creatures who could freely choose to love him and, as such, human beings are the only ones who can make that choice without being directly in the presence of God's power. It assumes humans are the reason for God having created in the first place.

While the following words are not found in the Bible, they are used by theologians to describe the importance of the creation of mankind. What does the dictionary say about them?

Apex

1. highest point: the highest point of something

2. most successful point: the most successful part of something, especially somebody's career or life

Culmination

1. highest point: the highest, most important, or final point of an activity

2. act of culminating: the arrival at, or the bringing of something to, a climax

Climax

1. vti reach key point: to reach the most important or exciting point in something such as an event or a story, or bring something to its most important or exciting point

Crown

1. top-ranking title: a title or distinction that signifies victory or supreme achievement

2. uppermost part: the top part of something, especially a hill

Now, does this suggest that the sole reason for creation was to create humankind? I think so, for according to the Bible, if the apex (or crown, or climax) of creation—humankind—was not created, then creation would not have been "good."

It Is Argued That Psalm 8 Says Otherwise

Some have argued that along with Psalm 8, Psalm 144:3 and the ending of Job show that man is insignificant, and that's true. But insignificant compared to what? Human beings are insignificant compared to God alone, but that says nothing against the idea that human beings are the apex of his creation. It's entirely consistent for man to be the reason for creation and at the same time for God to be so above mankind that the Psalmist can wonder why God even bothers with us.

Others argue, based upon Psalm 8, that human beings are "lower than angels." But this is clearly based upon an obvious mistranslation and a misinterpretation.

Let's take a good look at Psalm 8:3-8 (New American Standard Bible):

> When I consider Your heavens, the work of Your fingers,
> The moon and the stars, which You have ordained;

The Psalmist is not conceiving of the type of universe we do today, as we've seen...by far.

> What is man that You take thought of him,
> And the son of man that You care for him?

Notice this is a case of Hebrew parallelism for future reference below. The first phrase is paralleled by the second one, even though no parallel phrase is exactly similar in all respects. "Man = son of man"; "thought of" = "care for." This is basic wisdom literature exegesis here.

So if by the word "man" the Biblical writer thought of the phrase "son of man," then this same phrase, when applied to Jesus, must mean little more than what it means here. If, however, the phrase "son of man," when applied to Jesus, means "son of God," then all human beings should be considered "sons of God."

> Yet You have made him a little lower than God,
> And You crown him with glory and majesty!

Again, a Hebrew parallelism. God is crowned with unique glory and majesty that none other receives, so also God crowns man with glory and majesty no other creation receives.

In any case, Hebrews 2 is obviously a misinterpretation of this Psalm, since the Hebrew writer is speaking exclusively about Jesus as the "son of man" who was made lower than the angels by virtue of being born a man. In Psalm 8, it was humankind itself that was made lower than God. The author of Hebrews understood Psalm 8 primarily as messianic and eschatological. Yet there is no reason to read it as such in the Psalm itself...none! In Hebrews, not *mankind*, as in Psalm 8, but *Jesus* is awarded this dominion in the world to come. That the Hebrews author was not just now introducing this subject is made plain by the expression "about which we are speaking" in Heb. 2:5.

The Bible Knowledge Commentary: An Exposition of the Scriptures (2:784), has this to say about the thoughts of the writer of the Epistle to the Hebrews:

He was thinking here primarily of Jesus (Heb. 2:9). No doubt the familiar messianic designation "Son of Man" (v. 6) contributed to this understanding. Thus, he asserted, while total dominion over the created order is not yet His, Jesus is at last seen as crowned with glory and honor because He suffered death. The One so crowned was made a little lower than the angels for the very purpose of dying, that is, that by the grace of God He might taste death for everyone. This last statement is best understood as the purpose of the Lord's being made lower than the angels in His Incarnation.

If anyone else misinterpreted a text in this manner, Christians themselves would laugh at them. The only thing the Hebrews writer does say when comparing angels to mankind is this rhetorical question: "Are not all angels ministering spirits sent to serve those who will inherit salvation?" (Heb. 1:14). And this makes my point.

About Psalm 8:5, where it uses the word *Elohim* (translated "God" above), *The Bible Knowledge Commentary: An Exposition of the Scriptures* says this:[1]

> The KJV followed the Septuagint (LXX) in translating this word "angels." The NIV has chosen heavenly beings, which follows the same interpretation. Though in some cases *'ĕlōhîm* may refer to angels, this is not its main meaning. Man was created as God's own representative on earth, over the Creation, but lower than God. David was amazed that God should exalt finite man to such a place of honor.

There is no word for word equivalence between Hebrew and Greek words such that the LXX accurately represents the Hebrew *'ĕlōhîm*. Nonetheless, it is arguably illegitimate to base an interpretation on a Greek translation of a Hebrew word, just as it is to base a belief founded upon a misunderstanding of the context of a whole passage.

Evangelicals might want to affirm the fact that the author of Hebrews renders "*Elohim*" (gods) as "αγγελους" (angels) and that this suffices to clarify the meaning of the Psalm within biblical theology (Heb. 2:7). But this opinion is nothing different than saying this: "The Bible said it; I believe it; that settles it." Hebrews 2 is clearly based on a misinterpretation of the

---

[1] Walvoord, John & Zuck, Roy (1983), *The Bible Knowledge Commentary: An Exposition of the Scriptures by Dallas Seminary Faculty – Old* Testament, Colorado Springs: David C. Cook, p. 797.

text of Psalm 8 as well as a mistranslation of a word in it. The Hebrews writer used the Septuagint translation, which had already previously rendered *"Elohim"* as *"αγγελους."* Is the LXX inspired? Tell me! And does inspiration guarantee that what the Bible says is accurate even when it can clearly be shown to be incorrect? How is this possible?

Biblical scholar Hector Avalos informs me about the translation of *Elohim* and wrote this (via email):

> The translation of *'elohim'* as "god(s)" in Psalm 8:5 is not controversial anymore, and is accepted in the following translations:
>
> NRSV: "lower than God."
>
> REV: "less than a god"
>
> NAB: "less than a god"
>
> NJB: "less than a god."
>
> To be more literally accurate, 'less than the gods' would be better because *Elohim* is plural. This is also the opinion of Mitchell Dahood, the Catholic biblical scholar, in his commentary on the Psalms I:-1-50 (Anchor Bible; New York: Doubleday, 1965), p. 51. He translates it, "Yet you have made him a little less than the gods" (p. 48).
>
> Man was created a little lower than the gods, which reflects a polytheistic religious viewpoint. In order to soften the polytheistic implications of this the translators do some interesting things with this Hebrew word.

Returning to Psalm 8:3-8:

> You make him to rule over the works of Your hands;
> You have put all things under his feet,

Again, Hebrew parallelism. But notice the phrase "works of Your hands" here. That phrase can only parallel the earlier phrase "the work of Your fingers" in verse 3 above, and this refers to "the heavens," which include "the moon and the stars."

Only one evangelical conclusion about the central role of man can come from for a correct reading of Psalm 8: human beings are the highest creation, even above angels. Man is just a little lower than God himself. If God created angels they are below man.

> All sheep and oxen,
>
> And also the beasts of the field,
>
> The birds of the heavens and the fish of the sea,
>
> Whatever passes through the paths of the seas.

This is what the Psalmist thought all creation involved. It is crystal clear that he said mankind rules over all the works of God's hands earlier, and here he tells us what this means. There are no references to aliens or angels. Maybe he just didn't think they existed or that they just didn't compare to the status of mankind—it's hard to say exactly what he may have thought. But in either case, since the theists I write to believe this Psalmist was inspired to write God's words, then they have a problem with the scale of the universe, for this Psalm affirms what Genesis 1-2 and Romans 8 affirm that mankind is the apex of God's creation.

Even if angels are higher in status than mankind, they are not higher in status with regard to the creation of this universe, the *mundus* (physical creation). Angels are apparently like ghosts, not limited to the physical universe. We are not told when angels were created. Genesis speaks only about the universe of things that God supposedly created. And of them, mankind is the highest creation, the climatic reason for it all, which speaks directly to the issue of how large we should expect this physical universe to be.

Christians can object that God had other purposes in creating the universe. One such purpose in creating a universe that is old and vast is to demonstrate to them His power and sovereignty based upon what Paul says in Romans 1:20: "For since the creation of the world God's invisible qualities—his eternal power and divine nature—have been clearly seen, being understood from what has been made..."

Yes, this is indeed part of God's goal to be glorified, which is his preeminent goal above all goals according to Calvin. This just means that God has several goals: 1) To be glorified by 2) displaying his power and his love for his creation, and by 3) redeeming his human representatives from Satan and sin.

These are his main goals, and I don't deny them. These things are non-controversial. Romans 1:20 does not say that God's purpose in creation was to show his power, only that his power is seen in creation. And even given that God's goal was to display his power in creation, it still does not say anything about *how* God intended to display his power. It's clear in the Bible that God's power is seen best in redemption in his defeat of the mythical beast of Satan, along with sin in the lives of his human representatives, the only ones made in his image. It's very clear he created a world as a cosmic stage with man as the apex for this redemptive drama to unfold.

Some have suggested there might be other goals for God's having created this present universe, like "1) to get people to wonder if there is a God who made all of this; 2) to cause people to reflect on his glory and power (i.e., worship); 3) to humble us; 4) to show us how important we are to him, how much he cares, etc." But if my argument here is successful, then the scale of this universe is actually counterproductive to achieving these goals.

Here is a Powerful Analogy

Since theists are so fond of the parental analogy when it comes to the problem of evil, let me offer one that actually works when it comes to the scale of the universe. Let's say a great-great-great-great-great-grandfather makes a playhouse for his children to play in that is the size of the United States, which no one else is to use until they are born. And they learn through a last will and testament that he made it for them (evangelicalism). The playhouse was created expressly and exclusively for those children. In it are placed all kinds of animals. They have been living in it and reproducing and devouring one another since he placed them within. Birds, kittens, puppies, gerbils, hamsters, small turtles, along with various bugs...as well as all kinds of predators like lions, tigers, bears, spiders, scorpions, and snakes. They are told to do with it what they want (given a few rules as the creator/great-great...grandfather). It does not belong to anyone else.

These children would expect that this playhouse would be on a child's scale. They would not expect adult things in it, like lions, tigers and bears, high windows they cannot reach or see out, chasms they could not cross, levels they cannot reach, or areas they could not even see, much less even visit. This is what they should expect, and this is obviously so.

Now the great-great...grandfather might have reasons for doing otherwise than they expect, but what would they be? It is, after all, the child's playhouse, created on a child's scale. Not even other adults could figure out why a father would create an adult scaled playhouse for children, much less could the children themselves figure it out.

So this would quite naturally lead the children to question the intelligence or kindness of their great great...grandfather (since they cannot question his existence, which is what they would do if, like us, they never saw him). But in our case, with our universe, we *do* question the existence of God given our so-called playhouse, which was not created on a human scale.

God should have gotten down to the business of creating humans right away instead of wasting time on dinosaurs and saber-toothed tigers and woolly mammoths because of the amount of animal suffering that took place prior to the arrival of mankind. I see an obvious connection with my analogy here. It was a waste if man is the apex of creation, especially if there was so much needless suffering due to the law of predation in the natural world (which is morally baseless and unnecessary). Since there are no moral lessons for animals to learn from their sufferings, and since there is no reward for them in heaven after they die, that needless suffering demands an explanation.

Historical Evidence for These Expectations

I also think there is historical evidence that the church as a whole expected a smaller universe with the Earth at the center of it, although there are a few notable theologians who thought otherwise. The evidence from Christian history, based upon Biblical passages, is that they did in fact think the Earth was the center of a small universe with man the apex of creation.

An overwhelming number of Christians prior to the rise of modern science believed they were on a fixed planet in the center of a very small universe compared to what we have more recently found. Just see Dante's universe as depicted in his monumental poem, the *Divine Comedy*. This book was extremely influential in depicting the universe as it was believed to exist by the masses of Christians who hadn't been censored by the influential theologians and heresy hunters [see Diagram on the p. 142].

Dante's poem was hugely influential:

It is widely considered the pre-eminent work in Italian literature. and one of the greatest works of world literature. The poem's imaginative vision of the afterlife is representative of the medieval worldview as it had developed in the Western Church by the 14th century. It helped establish the Tuscan language, in which it is written, as the standardized Italian language. It is divided into three parts: Inferno, Purgatorio, and Paradiso.[1]

Dante's *Divine Comedy* was believed to depict the known universe. I don't think this can be reasonably denied. This is how they thought about the world. Take a good look at that universe. *That's what most people expected prior to having scientific knowledge.* As such, the force of my argument is related to what they expected. If most people expected something different than what was found then that's some pretty strong evidence for what Everett, Carrier and I argue for, which is contrary evidence to the Christian theistic hypothesis.

The church tried and convicted Galileo for his astronomical ideas and placed Galileo's book on the banned list. Descartes refused to publish his book "The World" after Galileo was arrested and tried. Does that not count as slowing down the progress of science? When it came to surgeries, the medical need for cadavers, and every *innovative* type of advance, I think Christianity either slowed the progress of science or tried to stop it. Remember, every *innovative* type of progress. Stem cell research is just a recent example. As the power of the church has declined, the successes of science have multiplied.

In fact, given the Galileo debacle as propagated by the *Philosophes* of an earlier day, precisely because God did not communicate to his people accurate information about the true size and scale of the universe, the Bible and the church lost credibility in the eyes of many people. The Galileo debacle has been used rightly or wrongly as disastrous for the credibility of the church and the Bible as a whole. Because God failed to tell us about the scale of the universe, it has led many to see the Bible as written by non-inspired superstitious people.

---

[1] "Divine Comedy," *Wikipedia*, https://en.wikipedia.org/wiki/Divine_Comedy (Accessed 26/05/2022).

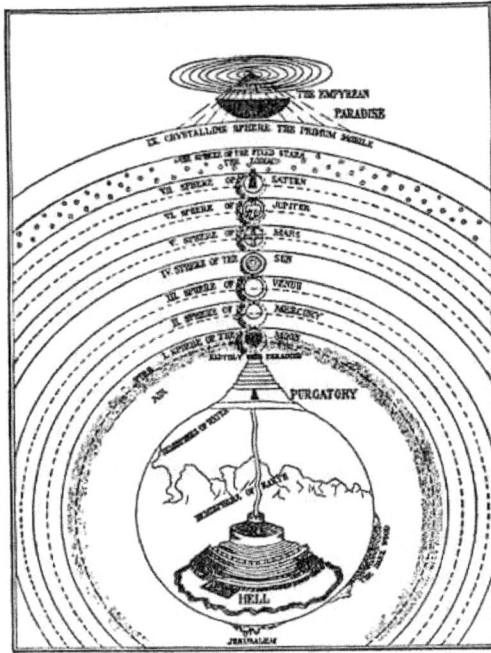

Figure 2: Michelangelo Caetani, 1855, La Materia della Divina Commedia di Dante Aligherie. The Structure of Dante's universe in "The Divine Comedy".

Some creationists, like astrophysicist Hugh Ross, claim God needed to create such a vast and old universe in order for the earth to exist with the right conditions to support human life as we know it. But this is the lamest argument of them all, in my opinion. Why? Because Ross and other Christian theists believe God is omnipotent such that he created the laws of the universe in the first place! So if God is this omnipotent deity and if he created the laws of the universe, then he could have merely created (given his omnipotence) a small planet containing human beings; and that's it.

This is just obvious to me. But even if I grant them their point, it doesn't even matter, for this same God is supposedly a miracle working God. Even if it was metaphysically impossible for God to create the Earth as it is without a vast universe because he couldn't create nature's laws differently, then this says nothing at all against God performing perpetual miracles. If he is a miracle working God, he could indeed have created a terrestrial biosphere that would sustain human life even if the laws of nature would not allow it. All it would take would be a few perpetual miracles. Such activity is supremely easy for an omnipotent god. As far as theists

142

know, the laws of nature are themselves just perpetual miracles created by God anyway.

Placing This Argument in a Larger Context

Finally, let me place this whole argument into a larger context. There is no good reason for God to have created anything at all, much less a universe so vast and old. As If God created a world, given his stated purposes in the Bible, it seems to me he would not create animals in the first place. As already mentioned, if he did, he wouldn't have them exist for hundreds of thousands of years before the apex of his creation came on the scene, especially since animals would not be "needed." Animals experience a great deal of suffering due to the law of predation, which is morally baseless and unnecessary. Moreover, there are no moral lessons for animals to learn from their sufferings, and there is no reward for them in heaven after they die. It just looks pointless.

This whole argument is but another example of where God did not communicate effectively to his people. He did not clearly and unequivocally condemn witch hunts (worse, see Ex. 22:18: "Thou shalt not suffer a witch to live"), Inquisitional trials and tortures leading to death, or brutal slavery. Nor did he condemn wars fought for religious causes (worse, he commanded them, e.g. Dt. 7 and Dt. 20:16-17), like the Crusades. Also, there is no clear prophecy that was stated prior to an event that clearly applies to a distant future event that cannot be chalked up to mere wishful thinking, or luck. God not only did *not* create our bodies with a stronger immune system, he didn't even give us instructions from the get-go on how to discover penicillin, much less even tell us that such a thing is possible and that we should look for it (because millions of people would needlessly die before we were to discover it). And that's just one such discovery.

There are so many things God did not tell us in advance that it sometimes amazes me Christians think that he exists. Let me just ask the believer to show me something, anything, even one thing, that we find in the Bible that could not have been spoken by an ancient person of his times, such that what he said could only be attributed to his having divine knowledge. It cannot be done. The evidence is that there is nothing in the Bible that could not have been said by a human being living in that day and time...*nothing*. The Bible is a human product coming from superstitious ancient people.

Christian responses to this problem are *ex post facto* ones, after the fact. They claim an omnipresent God didn't have to create a small universe or the Earth in its center. Sure, I understand their reasoning, *given after-the-fact explanations*, once the facts have been established. But what Everitt and I are talking about is what one would expect *beforehand*! Christians do the same thing with slavery. Most Christians today claim the Bible was clear about slavery and that slave holders in the American South were stupid about the Bible and immoral. But again, that's *ex post facto* reasoning too. There are many powerful Biblical passages that support what they believed about slavery, just as there are many powerful Biblical passages that support Dante's Universe. It's obvious that *ex post facto* arguments have little effect on this argument precisely because they are *ex post facto*. They are contrived to fit the data, but are not predicted explanations.

God did not tell us something about the scale of the universe. Any good all-knowing creator-god should have truthfully informed us about the world we live in, since if he truly is its creator, he should know more about it than he allegedly revealed. So when modern science discovered it, such a discovery undermined the credibility of the Bible and the church whose theology is based on it. By not revealing the truth about such a significant issue for modern people beforehand, he caused a massive amount of doubt for all future believers in the Bible.

This is one of the major reasons why I reject Christianity today. The Genesis creation accounts are myths. There is nothing in them about how or why the universe began to exist. If God existed, then he could have provided us with some truth about this. He didn't because the Bible is not from God.

My beef is not about whether or not the *Philosophes* properly understood the Galileo affair, but whether or not God would knowingly withhold information from his people knowing that, by doing so, he would be misleading them. And not just about the scale of the universe, but also misleading (or not correcting) people about witches and heretics and black people who had "The Curse of Ham." Any idiot would see potential problems about such things, much more so should an omniscient God. Why didn't God ever say, even just once, "Thou shalt not own, buy, sell, or trade human beings as slaves," let alone say it as often as needed?

So I think the *Argument From the Scale of the Universe*, especially when placed into this larger context, makes it "probably false" that evangelical Christianity is correct.

13 – The Scale of the Universe Undercuts the Belief in a Tribal Deity

Does the scale of the universe undercut the belief in a tribal deity? Yes, most emphatically, and that is what I hope to illustrate here.

First, we have to show that a tribal deity is what we find in the Bible. After that the rest is easy. A god like that, who is only concerned with a small tribe on a very large planet, must not know about the planet. Such a tribal deity looks indistinguishable from one created by a given tribe. Tribal deities were to be found everywhere tribes could be found. Since all of the rest of these deities were created by tribal people, then the odds are that the god of the Bible was created by the Israelite tribe.

What, then, of Anselm's omniscient, omnipotent, omnipresent God? What if this is the god who exists instead of a tribal deity? Does it change anything? No, I don't think so, not much anyway, although this is the point of contention. We would have to see the reasoning from the Bible's tribal deity to Anselm's God. Personally, I don't see it.

In fact, the biblical evidence is overwhelmingly against Anselm's God being the Bible's God. To the degree someone agrees with this assessment of the Bible then to that same degree the scale of the universe undercuts the belief in the tribal deity. It does so on a continuum, by degrees.

Let's say Anselm's God exists despite the Bible, that there exists an omniscient, omnipotent, omnipresent God anyway, who represents the Christian God despite that biblical evidence. Then what? At that point we'd have to look into the probability that such a deity can be a person, that he can exist without a body, that he can know what time it is in all parts of the universe, and that he can be everywhere an atom can be found. None of these things seem probable either. To the degree someone agrees with this assessment of Anselm's omni-God then to that same degree the scale of the universe undercuts the belief in Anselm's God.[1] It does so on a continuum, by degrees.

But even if these insoluble problems can be solved, there are two additional concerns. The first concern has to do with why Anselm's God should care about one pale blue dot in the universe with one kind of species in it. If the Gospels and Paul's writings are to be believed, then why would God be so concerned about one species of life on one pale blue dot enough to die for our sins so we could be in heaven? And why are our so-called sins so egregious to this God such that they will send non-believers to an everlasting punishment, when it appears no other life on our planet or in the universe faces this same threat? These things don't seem probable either, since we don't see any evidence that Anselm's God cares for anything, given natural and morally caused suffering in the world. To the degree someone agrees with this assessment of Anselm's God then to that same degree the scale of the universe undercuts the belief in Anselm's God. It does so on a continuum, by degrees.

The second concern has to do with the need for Anselm's God to create a universe on the scale we find. If this universe was created for the purpose of human life and the central redemptive act took place here, then the rest of the universe and life itself seems unnecessary at best. And if this universe is only a temporary testing ground for the heavenly reality, which is more important and everlasting, then it seems like a lot of wasted energy even if an omnipotent God exists. It doesn't seem probable that Anselm's God did this since he could have done anything else, even creating a flat earth and hanging stars in the sky, which would be just a few miles above the clouds as the ancients believed. It doesn't seem probable such a God would create the universe on such a large scale when we consider the skepticism it has produced in the minds of scientifically literate people either. To the degree someone agrees with this assessment of Anselm's God then to that same degree the scale of the universe undercuts the belief in Anselm's God. It does so on a continuum, by degrees.

Now, what if we combine these objections against Anselm's God? Let's say we don't see the Bible as supporting such a deity, nor do we see how such a deity can be a person, that he can exist without a body, that he

---

[1] For a greater substantiation of the arguments against the Anselmian God, see Chapter 2 of my book *Unapologetic*. [Loftus, John (2016), *Unapologetic*, Durham, NC: Pitchstone Publishing.]

can know what time it is in all parts of the universe, and that he can be everywhere there is an atom. And let's also say we don't see any evidence Anselm's God cares for anything given natural and morally caused suffering in the world, nor that such a God would create such a huge universe knowing it would produce the very kind of scientific skepticism of his existence that has resulted. And let's say these are overriding factors to quite a large degree. Then the scale of the universe does indeed undercut Anselm's God in a cumulative fashion by degree.

One might think of it this way. Take, for instance, the existence of witchcraft. Technically speaking, we cannot conclusively prove that a Devil or his demons do not exist, or that witches cannot work their magic. There just isn't any evidence that they do. Furthermore, with the advancement of science, supernatural explanations for any given event in our lives become unnecessary and superfluous. A Devil-empowered witch may have caused a particular illness by her spell. But what best explains why we can usually trace the illness to some undercooked food that was eaten, as an example? And what best explains why the right medicine always cures the illness? If an illness was caused by the spell of a witch, there is no reason to think we could find a natural cause for it. Nor is there a reason to think the right medicine could always overcome the power of the spell by curing it either.

Technically speaking, we cannot say the scale of the universe *proves* that Anselm's deity does not exist either. But with these additional concerns, the fact of the scale of the universe *does* lead us to think such a deity is an unnecessary hypothesis indistinguishable from the non-existence of such a God.

When I was in the throes of doubt in the early 90s, I bought nearly a dozen poster pictures of galaxies, stars, various nebula, and the solar system itself. I hung them on the walls of my office. I was astounded by our universe and its massive size. I read a few astronomy books, too. Science tells us so much about our universe.

I remember thinking to myself how God could be omnipresent in such a universe, how he could be a personal agent without a center for his personality in it, how he could be omniscient knowing what was going on at the far reaches of it, and how he could be omnipotent such that he could create and maintain it. I also wondered how he could care about life on this pale blue dot of ours that exists on one spiral arm in the Milky Way galaxy. What kind of God could exist, given this universe? How could he interact with parts of it several billions of light years away when a light year is a measurement of both time and distance? I had already come to think God was located in time in some sense, ever since the creation. So how could such a God act in the present here on Earth and also several billions of light years away in a different part of the universe? Does that even make sense?

In the ancient world, all civilizations that we know of thought their particular city or territory was the center of the Earth, and so they built temples as earthly homes for their gods for when they came down from the sky (heaven). Then, when people learned of the size of the Earth, they believed it was the center of things. When people found that the sun was the center of the solar system, the solar system was believed to be the center of things (not the sun, which would have been logical). When we found ourselves to be on a spiral arm of the Milky Way galaxy, things changed again, especially with the fact that there is no center to the universe of billions of galaxies.

So what makes me think the size of the universe leads to atheism? Everything I just mentioned, all of it and more left unspecified, since this is just a brief chapter. I think it's even more damaging when it comes to an omnipotent God who supposedly created the universe for the specific purpose of gaining the affections of people on this lone planet of ours. If this is what he desired (for some irrational egotistical reason), he could have simply created us on a flat disk in a much smaller universe like the one the ancients believed existed. The size of the universe is even more damaging to the god we find in the Bible, a tribal deity with a body,[1] one of the members of a pantheon of gods, which included a wife and sons. Hey, we know he had sons,[2] so we know he also had a wife.

---

[1] See Stavrakopoulou, Francesca, *God: An Anatomy*, New York: Knopf.
[2] Genesis 6:4-2; Jeremiah 31:9; Job 1:6; Deuteronomy 32:8; etc. Also, in Canaanite literature, the god El begot 70 sons with Asherah, known as the "council of El," as seen in Psalms 82:1-6; 138:1; 29:1; 89:7.

14 - Pascal's Wager Revisited

In my previous book *Why I Became an Atheist,* I dealt with Pascal's Wager in chapter 3. The wager goes something like this:

Either (a) there is a God who will send only the religious people to heaven or (b) there is not. To be religious is to wager for (a). To fail to be religious is to wager for (b). We can't settle the question whether (a) or (b) is the case, for if God exists, he is infinitely incomprehensible to us. But (a) is clearly vastly better than (b). With (a) infinite bliss is guaranteed, while with (b) we are still in the miserable human condition of facing death with no assurance as to what lies beyond. We must wager; it is not optional. So (a) is clearly the best wager: if we gain, we gain all; if we lose, we lose nothing.

I want to share three of the main criticisms of it in what follows. There is the evidential objection, the gambler's objection, and the many gods objection.

The evidential objection concerns how much evidence Christianity should have before I must take seriously the claims of Christianity. Keep in mind that Pascal's Wager is a purely prudential argument that is supposed to help us decide what to do when the evidence is inclusive. It's meant as a tiebreaker when someone cannot decide between skepticism and Christianity. The Christianity referred to in this argument is of the conservative branches. It's meant to defend the type of Christianity that promises an everlasting conscious torment in a fiery hell. Other types of Christianity don't even apply, those affirming annihilation, or universal salvation, since there isn't much to fear if one is wrong.

In any case, I judge that conservative Christianity has about a .00001% probability of being correct, or 1 in 100,000. This is something I think one can conclude from the arguments in all of my books. Given that I might be wrong in this judgment, since I've been wrong before, I'll up it to a .0001% probability of being correct, or 1 in 10,000. This probability has nothing to do with how many other religions and gods there are. It's a probability based solely on the merits of the evidence and arguments themselves. Others will judge this case differently, of course. So my argument precludes Pascal's Wager because we do not need a tie breaker. The evidence is against the Christian claim, decisively.

Keep in mind what this means. It means that there is a 99.99% probability that Christianity is delusional. [It also means that unless there is a religion with a greater amount of probability then there is a .0001% chance this life is all there is]. This makes Pascal's Wager an argument a force akin to someone crying "wolf," or someone else yelling "the sky is falling." Why should I take the bet if I see no credibility in the warning?

Still, perhaps Pascal's wager has a good deal of force, the evidential objection alone notwithstanding, since the payout is an infinite amount with an eternal bliss if correct. But the force of it, if there is any, will only apply to people who like to gamble, who like taking risks for the sake of taking risks, who don't mind the low odds for a high payout—an eternal bliss.

This brings us to the second objection, which I call **the gambler's objection**. There are two types of gamblers. There are risk-taking ones who love the thrill of betting, just to bet, and then there are reasonable gamblers. When it comes to the risk-taking gambler there would be nothing we could say if she wanted to take a risk and gamble against Pascal's Wager, even granting Pascal's argument. After all, such a person is a gambler who takes risks. Such a gambler could still bet fifty/fifty against an eternal bliss by living life as she pleases, in hopes Pascal is wrong!

Let me focus on reasonable gamblers. Anyone who plays the very popular poker game called *Texas Hold'em*, for instance, knows what I'm talking about when I say there is a distinction to be made between the actual odds and the pot (or money) odds. *Actual odds* are the mathematical odds of someone's poker hand winning the pot. The *pot odds* concern the ratio of the amount of a particular bet to the total money in the pot at the time of that bet. If, say, someone must bet $5 in hopes of winning the pot, which has $200 in it, then the pot odds are 40 to 1, which is the ratio of the money in the pot to the bet ($200 divided by $5). For every dollar the gambler bets with such odds, she has the potential of winning $40. Such a bet is a good one even if the actual mathematical odds of winning the hand are not large, because the risk is small in comparison to the reward. If, on the other hand, someone must place a bet of $50 to win the same pot of $200 (or a ratio of 4 to 1 pot odds), the bet is a bad one unless the actual odds of winning the hand are much greater, for the reward is not worth the risk.

Let's say the two cards you've been dealt with are two spades, an Ace and a King. Let's also assume that of the four other cards dealt face up on the poker table two of them are also spades (say, 5 and 8). At that point you need for the last dealt card to be either an ace (winning pair of aces) or a king (winning pair of kings), or a spade (for a winning spade flush). The actual odds of one of those cards being drawn last are a little better than 1 in 3. Let's assume that if one of these cards is dealt last, you'll win that poker hand. Let's also assume you must decide whether or not to place a bet of $4 on a pot that has $36 in it before that last card is dealt face up on the table. That's 36 divided by 4 equals 9; or 9 to 1 pot odds. At that point you must ask yourself whether you should place that $4 bet. The actual odds are against you 1 to 3, but the pot odds are in your favor 9 to 1. Because of the pot odds, you should bet the $4, and here's why: If you faced this same situation seventy-five times and bet $4 each time for a total of $300, and you won one time out of three bets (the actual odds), your gain would be about $900 because of the pot odds.

Now let's consider the actual odds and the pot odds when it comes to Pascal's Wager. According to the Wager the payout is an infinite amount, so the pot odds are extremely high; an eternal bliss. With the pot odds so extremely high, it's argued I should place the bet. And what are we to bet? According to the Christian faith I must bet it all, my whole life. I must die daily. I must take up my cross and follow Jesus. I must be totally committed and have total faith. That's what I'm called upon to do, daily, even to the point of guarding my very thoughts. I must sacrifice that which I think about—I should not lust, hate, covet, nor entertain any doubts.

But here's the problem. Good poker players only place reasonable bets. That's what makes them good poker players in the first place. And they win more often than people who don't place reasonable bets, even if a risk-taking gambler might get lucky once in a while with an unreasonable bet. Hence, this is the key to winning at poker—only placing reasonable bets.

What makes any bet based on high pot odds a reasonable one? In the first place, placing a bet based on the pot odds is only a reasonable one if the poker player plays a certain number of hands. It's the number of hands that she plays that makes a bet based on the pot odds a reasonable one. As indicated above, placing a bet on the actual odds of 1 to 3 with the pot odds being 9 to 1 is a good bet precisely because the poker player will continue to play more hands of poker. As she does, she will eventually win more money—it's all but guaranteed! But if we are only going to play one hand of poker and we never play the game again, then a reasonable bet must be made on the actual odds (the higher the better), otherwise, the person making such a bet is nothing more nor less than a gambler who simply likes the thrill of taking bigger and bigger risks for bigger and bigger rewards.

Secondly, reasonable poker players should never gamble more than they can afford to lose, even if the odds are fifty/fifty. A poker player must consider the impact of losing everything she has when placing a bet. Even if someone might think gamblers are not being unreasonable by wagering everything they own, what reason would we say that a non-gambler should place this bet if the actual odds are fifty/fifty? Who, for instance, would say it's a reasonable bet to flip a coin in the air with a fifty-fifty chance of winning when a person must bet everything she owns, including his $350,000 house, $50,000 car, and her very livelihood, for a chance of having the riches equal to everyone in the world, making people like Bill Gates and heads of state like those of Saudi Arabia paupers by comparison? While some people may indeed place this bet, it's certainly not a reasonable one demanded of everyone. The non-gambler whose life is happy has no reason to risk that which she already has for that which could be hers. And while we'd think the person who lost this bet was foolish, anyone who won it would also be foolish, even though they won. They would only be lucky. For this reason, poker players do not bet everything they've got unless they are pretty sure they have a winning hand. Pot odds are minimized as a factor with a bet like this.

So if the actual odds for a winning poker hand in *Texas Hold'em* are 1 in 3, it does not matter what the pot odds are if this is the player's last hand and if she must bet everything she has! Pot odds only matter when the gambler can play a number of hands and when she's not betting everything she owns. So when it comes to Pascal's Wager how many times can a religious seeker bet everything for the chance of winning the eternal bliss pot? She can only do this one time! And she must bet everything. There are no second chances. There are no more hands to play. This would be it.

Since contrary to Pascal, I calculate the actual odds at much less than fifty/fifty, and since contrary to Pascal, I consider my life to be happy just the way it is, and since this is the only hand I will ever be able to bet on, I must bet on the actual odds. Therefore, accepting Pascal's Wager is simply a very bad bet. The actual odds are extremely low for his bet. With those odds I will undoubtedly lose everything I have...my present life!

The third objection to Pascal's Wager is the decisive one, **the many gods objection**. It eliminates the force of Pascal's wager, I think, since now we have many religions and many gods all clamoring for our obedience: Muslims, Mormons, Jehovah's Witnesses, and so on, and so forth.

One religion claims that if you don't follow its god you will fry in hell, while another one makes the same claim. Since many gods are threatening us with hell if we don't believe, then Pascal's Wager cannot help us to decide *between them*. All of them offer an infinite payout, too. All of them demand belief and obedience. Whom should we believe? Whom should we obey? Pascal's Wager does not answer this objection on its own terms. We still must judge which religious viewpoint has the most probability and such judgments are generally based on the accidents of birth, as I've argued with the *Outsider Test for Faith*. Hence Pascal's wager fails...badly.

15 – Can Prayer Change the Past?

At the present time, there is an interesting discussion among physicists about the possibilities of time travel, backward causation, and wormholes, leading them to think there is no longer anything standing in the way of changing the past. Time's arrow is no longer thought of as going in one direction. Quantum mechanics along with the Special and General Theories of Relativity allow for it. According to the Special Theory of Relativity, for instance, time is relative to the speed of an observer. As an observer approaches the speed of light, time slows down. With the possibility of time travel particles called *tachyons* (that travel faster than the speed of light, thus reversing time), time travel is possible along with changing the past. It may not be feasible to us, of course, but what about the feasibility of God doing so, if he exists?

With this understanding I propose a mutually agreed-upon scientific test for petitionary prayer. It must be a mutually agreed-upon test, by both atheists and theists, or else one side won't accept it as a true scientific test for prayer.

Christians claim God answers petitionary prayer. If a petitionary prayer comes to pass, then that prayer counts as evidence that their God exists and he answers prayer. If it doesn't come to pass, then they can claim it wasn't God's will to answer that prayer. Either way, they win.

I believe, however, that petitionary prayer can be scientifically tested. The test is simple. If God exists and if he has foreknowledge, then he can foreknow the prayers of believers. If God answers prayers and if believers pray to change tragic events of the past, then God can either change the past, or he can foreknow these prayers and prevent the past from happening as events take place. So, I have challenged people who believe in petitionary prayer to change the past. If they cannot do this, then either God does not exist, or God does not have foreknowledge. A third possible alternative is that God is not preventing the past from happening because believers are not praying about the past, but with this challenge of mine, that can change.

To believers who are hesitant to pray for the past I want to ask them a simple question: Do you believe God can prevent events in the past from happening based upon his foreknowledge of your prayers today? Yes or No? If yes, then pray. What's the harm? I'll bet most believers have prayed for something in the past anyway. They'll pray for events that have already taken place. A believer will pray that a child safely arrived at her destination all day long until he hears that she did. If that child is supposed to arrive by plane in Dallas at 9:10 a.m., believers will continue to pray for a safe arrival until they hear from someone that the child arrived, even though they might not hear about it for a few hours later. But if the child already arrived safely, then it would make no sense to expect God to answer any prayers after the fact. This is true even if the child did not arrive safely. For if the plane crashed at 9 a.m., all prayers for the safe arrival of the child after 9 a.m. are pointless, unless God can prevent, or change the past. So all prayers for the safe arrival of that child should stop when that child either arrives safely or she doesn't, unless believers expect God to do something about the past.

My challenge is to have Christians pick any tragic event in the past that everyone believes took place, announce that they are praying to change it, and then watch what happens. They must announce it in advance of praying for it, lest they claim to have changed tragic events that no one ever believed took place in the first place. It's a simple test. It could be to prevent the Holocaust, the terrorist 9/11 attacks, the assassination of John F. Kennedy, or any tragic event reported in the daily newspaper. My prediction is that the past will never be changed *and* that every prayer to change the past will be remembered by the one who prayed it precisely because nothing will ever change, ever. Every single one of them. Without fail. I claim that this should be considered strong evidence that either God does not exist, or that he does not have foreknowledge, however conceived. Choose any event and let's them begin. Get millions of Christians to pray. If that doesn't work, pick another tragic event...then another...then another. My prediction is that nothing will ever change. Nothing.

Believers might respond that God doesn't answer all prayers, but what can they say if God doesn't answer any of these prayers at all? Believers might also claim that we should not test God. However, Moses asked for evidence that God would be with him to lead the Israelites out of slavery (Exodus 4), Gideon asked for evidence that God would help him conquer the Midianites (Judges 6), and the prophet Malachi challenged believers to test God with their tithes (Malachi 3:10). According to the Bible there is nothing wrong with asking for evidence to believe. Even if some believers still want to maintain that they should not test God, my challenge need not be seen by them to be a test at all. For if God can either change the past, or prevent the past from happening based upon his foreknowledge of their prayers, then they should pray to change tragic events in the past simply to help alleviate the sufferings of people who lived in the past. Moreover, since believers typically think prayer is more efficacious when there are more believers praying for something, then they should get together to pray to have God prevent a tragic event in the past from taking place. I'm merely saying that believers should pray for the past just like they do for the future, since there is no reason why God can't answer prayers for the past. And in both cases, they can end their prayers with the words, "Thy will be done," too.

There are certain conceptions of God that this test will have a great deal of force against. If a believer thinks God exists outside of time, as Boethius did, then God can actually change what we consider to be the past based upon his knowledge of the prayers of believers (there would be no time indexed prefix "fore" to this knowledge of God's because he would be present for all events timelessly). Actually, with this conception of God there is no reason why God cannot change any event in the past, even without someone praying to change it. What reasons God might have for doing this I cannot specify. But Christians who believe in petitionary prayer typically think God acts based upon their prayers. Why else does Jesus tell them to pray that God would send forth workers into the harvest, unless God won't do that if they don't (Matthew 9:37-38)? Abraham purportedly argued God out of destroying all of the inhabitants of Sodom and Gomorrah (Genesis 18), while Moses purportedly argued God out of destroying the Israelites (Numbers 14). There is also a parable of Jesus, in which an unjust judge answered a request because a persistent widow kept pleading her case (Luke 18). This parable is meant to teach believers that they should continue to pray for God to alleviate their sufferings, and not give up.

There are certain conceptions of foreknowledge that this argument will have a great deal of force against. If a believer is a Molinist, then his God would know what believers would be praying for regardless of whether the event actually occurred yet. Based upon God's counter-factual knowledge of future free-willed contingent actions, he could intervene to prevent tragic events regardless of whether these events have occurred or not. Based upon this foreknowledge, God could answer these, as yet, unspoken prayers, by preventing the events before they occurred.

But this argument has force against any Christian theist who be-lieves God has foreknowledge. For if God foreknows the prayers of believers, then God should be able to prevent the past based upon his fore-knowledge of these future prayers.

Some Objections

One objection is that the past is already the result of God's actions in the past based upon his foreknowledge of the all the prayers of believers, both past, present, and future. If God were to change the past, or prevent the past from happening, he has already done it. If he did so in light of his fore-knowledge of our prayers, and he doesn't change his mind, then the past cannot be changed.

Let's make a distinction between A) history as we now know it, and B) History as it will forever be. History as we know it, A, is the history of events as we know them to have happened in the past. History as it will forever be, B, is final history never to be changed. For all we know there only exists A, history as we now know it. But what history ends up being B, as the result of the prayers of believers, is a different thing entirely. Until God pur-portedly ends human history and, with it, time itself, history as we know it, A, is always amendable due to the prayers of the saints and based upon God's foreknowledge of those prayers. If history can be changed, then the believer cannot say this particular history is the will of God. He can only say that about final history, i.e., the history that goes unchanged.

Of course, I see no reason why God cannot change his mind based upon petitionary prayer, as we've seen with Moses and Abraham earlier. There are many passages about God changing directions as the direct result of the actions and prayers of believers in the Bible, for instance. God is de-scribed as changing his mind in several passages in the Bible (Genesis 6:6-7; Exodus 32:10; Deuteronomy 9:13; I Samuel 15:11; Psalms 106:44-45; Jer-emiah 18:8-10; Joel 2:13; Amos 7:3, and Jonah 3:10). And if that is true, then I see no reason why it's not equally true that prayers to change the past might help to change God's mind. I see no reason why the past is fixed and unalterable, given the present state of physics, as I mentioned, and I like-wise see no reason why God cannot change the past if he is outside of time.

But even if it isn't possible to change God's mind about the past, what believers pray for can affect the past. All I'm referring to when arguing about prayer changing an event in the past is that prayer would be changing what God foreknows, since he supposedly has foreknowledge of the future. Christian philosophers such as George Mavrodes thinks the past can be altered and argues that whenever he does something then he also prevents God from ever having foreknown that he didn't do it. ["Is the Past Unpreventable" *Faith and Philosophy* Vol. 1, no. 2, (April 1984).

Whether the past can be changed really isn't the issue here anyway, since I'm talking about whether God could prevent an event from happening before it occurred based upon his foreknowledge of a future petitionary prayer. Here is where the argument has some force to it. According to George Mavrodes we prevent God from knowing something with every free choice we make. Since God cannot foreknow what we do if we don't do it, we must do it for him to know that we did. When we do, it prevents God from knowing we did otherwise. So we prevent God from knowing everything we don't do.

If Mavrodes is correct that when he does something he also prevents God from ever having foreknown that he didn't do it, then the prayers spoken after a tragic event can be answered if and only if believers actually pray. By praying, believers alter what God knows in the past, namely God's foreknowledge of what they do. In other words, if God can only foreknow what a believer does, then he can only retroactively answer prayers spoken after a tragic event if and only if they actually pray to change that event. If they don't pray, then there are no prayers for God to retroactively answer.

Believers purportedly "change" or "alter" or "prevent" or "determine" the past every single day by what they do. What do they "change" or "alter" or "determine," according to Mavrodes? They determine what God foreknows by their actions, and prayer is something they do. But God cannot foreknow what a believer does if he or she doesn't do it. So they must do it to alter the past, specifically what God knows about our future actions. By praying after a tragic event occurred in the past believers are purportedly determining what God foreknows from all eternity. And based upon his foreknowledge God can purportedly prevent the past from happening before it happens. The problem is that since God can only foreknow what believers do, he supposedly also foreknows that they won't be praying for a particular event to be changed. But if they do pray then God would have this foreknowledge.

Another objection has to do with the paradox of time loops, where philosophers are debating whether or not someone can actually go back in time and kill themselves. Or in our case, if a believer would pray that he died rather than his daughter in a car accident. But I see no reason why God couldn't answer that prayer, if a believer offered it, regardless of the time loop, for according to believers, the one praying that prayer is resurrected so that he would still remember offering that prayer. And as such, he really did pray that prayer. Several suggestions have been offered about these types of paradoxes. Perhaps God wouldn't answer those types of prayers, anyway. However, the notion of backward causation does not involve time loops. Backward causation simply is the claim that time can move in both directions, into the future as well as back in the past. If an event causes something to happen in the future there is no time loop, just as if an event that caused something in the past does not. It just means that something in the future caused something in the past. In our case, it merely means that God prevented an event in the past from happening, which was "caused" by the future prayers of the believer.

The most serious objection is probably that if God did decide to prevent an event in the past based upon his foreknowledge of the future prayers of believers, then no one would know God changed that event. That's a good argument, since all knowledge about an event, even the prayers themselves, would no longer exist. There would supposedly be no memory of those spoken prayers too. Let's say believers prayed to change the 9/11 terrorist attacks and God foreknew these prayers and prevented it. Then we wouldn't have any knowledge of that event or the fact that anyone prayed to change it, since we would be on a different time line. That is, the belief that God does not answer prayers is unfalsifiable.

However, I see no reason why God couldn't allow the believer who prayed to remember that he had prayed, so he could know his prayer was answered, and I see no reason why people whose future is unaffected by the event's not occurring couldn't still have knowledge that they had prayed to prevent it. And it is in this regard that I can still ask why no believer has ever claimed to have had such a prayer answered. Although, I'll admit that if a believer did claim to have changed the past because of a prayer, and if I had no memory of that event ever occurring in the first place, I would not think his claim is a credible one.

Let's assume God does answer a prayer to change the past, and the prayer is that a loved one does not die in a car crash a month ago. On this new timeline a believer never remembers praying the request because the loved one never died. At that point why would a believer care whether he remembers it or not? Would anyone? No. Why? Because his loved one is still alive. So why not pray, even if the results could never be shown to be positive? It shouldn't matter to believers, if all they can say is that we won't remember having prayed for an event if God answered your prayer. If that's their only objection, then they have no objection to praying for the past. If prayers can help the sufferings of someone in the past, and the past can be altered or changed, then Christian should have an obligation to pray for events in the past.

Even if I grant that we probably wouldn't know if God answers such a prayer, it doesn't change anything. For we could still know if God didn't answer such a prayer. And that's the point of this test. My bet is that God won't answer any such prayer, and that we will know this. My challenge is that believers can select and pray for every single tragic event in the past, and nothing will ever change. Not one. The believer will remember praying for something to change in the past because no prayer will ever change anything in the past.

We never have to be bothered with how we would know of it if such a prayer worked. Why? Because it will never work. That's my prediction. Have believers pray for 100 events of the past, anywhere from Lincoln's assassination to Jeffery Dahmer's victims. Write them down. 100 events. I predict that after praying there will still be 100 unchanged events on their list. They can say we wouldn't know it if God did answer such prayer all they want to, but there are still 100 events on that list. Or 1000 events. Or 1 million events. Depending upon how many events they prayed for, they will all still be there. That's my prediction.

You cannot conclude God answered some of these requests but that we just don't know that he did. Why? Because these events are still on their list. So pick any tragic event in the past. Announce it. Pray for it. And we'll never see God answering that prayer no matter how many times it is prayed for, and no matter how many believers are praying for it.

And when prayer is tested in this manner it *always fails! Always.*

As far as backward causation itself goes, and the potential unreality of time goes, there is a great deal of literature on this topic with quantum mechanics, wormholes, and *tachyons*. Backward causation is consistent with the theory of Special Relativity.

Time is not fixed according to the current state of physics. Many conclude from this that time is unreal. And if this is the case with your creator's world, then he himself can change the past even after it took place. There is nothing standing in God's way from doing so, since it already can (and probably does) take place. You can also do a search for wormholes, time travel, tachyons, backward causation, Omniscience and Free will, Special Theory of Relativity, Quantum Mechanics. There is an interesting book out called *Time's Arrow*. Time doesn't just move in one direction.

Now just apply this physics to God. If he foreknows prayers then he can not only change the past, with all of the strangeness that might go with it, but he can also prevent the past. If God is outside of time, then prayers for the past are just as likely to be heard and answered as prayers for the future.

It doesn't matter if praying to change the past wasn't mentioned in the Bible, either. There are many things we have realized with the advance of modern medicine and morality that we do differently because we know better that aren't mentioned in the Bible. What does the Bible say about nuclear war, abortion, assisted suicide, contraception, heart transplants, capital punishment, suing another Christian in today's denominational world, and so on and so on. Christians use Biblical principles to understand these things not explicitly condemned in the Bible.

Maybe through contemporary science God is leading a new generation of prayer warriors to pray for the past like never before? Why not?

The only problem Christians have with it is that they don't think it will work, and they won't admit it. Christian, you don't really believe in prayer after all, do you? That's what I think, and for good reason. Prayer doesn't work, period.

16 – *Psychic Epistemology*: The Special Pleading of William Lane Craig

My focus in this chapter is to expose the special pleading of philosopher and theologian William Lane Craig's *Psychic Epistemology* (or *Spirit-Guided Epistemology*) as I correctly call it—rather than *Reformed Epistemology* as it's known.

All apologetics is special pleading. If you want to be a Christian apologist you must perfect this art. Special pleading is an informal fallacy where someone uses a double-standard in assessing similar types of claims, by favoring one's own preference over others, *without providing a justifying reason for the double-standard*. Christian apologists are special pleading when using an outsider's perspective to assess other religious faiths, while using an insider's perspective to assess their own faith, *without providing a justifying reason for the double-standard.*[1]

I know a bit more about William Lane Craig's apologetics than most people, having majored under him for a Master of Theology degree (Th.M., 1985) at Trinity Evangelical Divinity School. One class I took under him in the Winter of 1984 was on "Plantinga's Thought." In it Craig introduced students to Christian philosopher Alvin Plantinga's works so far, in which he supported his *Psychic Epistemology*. So it's clear to me Craig knows he's using a double-standard in assessing different religious faiths, favoring his own sect-specific Christian faith over all others. He simply believes he has a justifying reason for the double-standard. It's found in his alleged inner witness of a disembodied publicly undetectable (holy) *Spirit Guide* from "the other side."

---

[1] An outsider has a non-believing agnostic perspective, whereas an insider has one specific religious perspective. See Loftus, *The Outsider Test for Faith: How to Know Which Religion is True* (Prometheus Books, 2013).

How Does William Lane Craig Know Christianity Is True?

Craig tries to make a distinction between how he *knows* Christianity is true from how he *shows* others that Christianity is true. He says he *knows* Christianity is true by a (holy) Spirit Guide, just as a psychic *knows* s/he has been contacted by "the other side." When it comes to *showing* Christianity is true, Craig uses philosophical arguments for the existence of his god, along with alleged testimonial evidence for the resurrection of Jesus from the dead. In other words, Craig admits his attempts to *show* Christianity is true are all a sham, a ruse, a mere debating tactic just to win for *show*, since he, along with every other Christian, already *knows* Christianity is true by a *Spirit Guide*.

To *show* this, Craig offers some *analogies*.[1] In one of them, Craig argues he might legitimately say he *knows* he didn't commit a crime, even though he cannot *show* twelve jurors that he's innocent. He personally *knows* he didn't do the crime despite the fact sufficient objective evidence *shows* he's guilty.

Even though cases like this one are real, it is *disanalogous* and even disingenuous for Craig to claim he *knows* what took place in ancient history based on a *Spirit Guide*, rather than on the efforts of historians who utilize the standard of reasonable evidential verification. If the historical evidence isn't conclusive, it is unreasonable to punt to the vices of faith in order to leap over wherever the probabilities stop.

---

[1] Craig and Plantinga throw up a lot of different analogies like these. Some of them purport to show there are things we *know* to be true based on personal experiences that only we have had, which we cannot in turn *show* (or prove) to others. Some other analogies purport to show there are things we *know* to be true without any proof or evidence. They argue by analogy that if these types of analogies succeed, then by extension Christians can legitimately believe in their god along with his revelation, even though they cannot in turn *show* (or prove) to others. In one analogy, since believing there are other minds is rational without evidence, so also is belief in their god.

The major problem with them is that possibilities don't count. Only probabilities do. It may be remotely possible we're living in the Matrix right now, or dreaming, or being deceived by an evil demon. But I'm not changing anything I do or anything I think based on a possibility. We must think exclusively in terms of the probabilities. I've concluded that all of these scenarios are disanalogous to believing in a god who acted in history. The only reasonable way to know that a god acted in history is for it to be based on sufficient historical evidence. Barring that, no one should believe a god acted in history. For more see Loftus, "The Demon, Matrix, Material World, and Dream Possibilities", *Internet Infidels*, https://infidels.org/kiosk/article/the-demon-matrix-material-world-and-dream-possibilities/, (Accessed 10/14/2022).

The accurate analogy is not Craig's innocent man, but rather jurors who determine someone's guilt based on reading their tea leaves in the morning, or by consulting a psychic. No one should think doing *that* is reasonable. So likewise, Craig cannot *know* that a snake or donkey talked, or that a guy named Moses forced the Egyptian Pharaoh of his day to release two million slaves who escaped across the bottom of a Red Sea, or that a virgin gave birth to a god's incarnate son, or that this same divine child arose from the dead because a *Spirit Guide* told him so, alleged to be "holy" or not, alleged to be spoken by a psychic or not, alleged to be a god or not. Craig's own scriptures warn him that "even Satan disguises himself as an angel of light" (2 Corinthians 11:14). Once someone believes in Satan then all bets are off the table.[1] For all Craig and Plantinga know, Satan may be the one inspiring them to accept *Psychic Epistemology,* and with it their sect-specific conservative religion, which is false and has harmed great numbers of people.[2]

Nonetheless, Craig says he *knows* the miraculous events in the Bible happened because of the witness of a (holy) *Spirit Guide.* Craig says this witness is "self-authenticating." What does he mean by that? "I mean that the witness, or testimony, of the Holy Spirit is its own proof; it is unmistakable; it does not need other proofs to back it up; it is self-evident and attests to its own truth." Hitchhiking on the philosophical work of Alvin Plantinga's defense of a properly basic belief in God,[3] and quote-mining the Bible (e.g., John 14:16-26; 16:7-11; Gal. 3:26; 4:6; 8:15-16; 1 John 2:20, 26-27; 3:24; 5:7-10), Craig writes, "I would agree that belief in the God of the Bible is a properly basic belief, and emphasize that it is the ministry of the Holy Spirit that supplies the circumstance for its proper basicality. And because this belief is from God, it is not merely rational, but definitely true."[4]

---

[1] On this see Johnson, David Kyle (2017), "Justified Belief in the Existence of Demons Is Impossible", in *Philosophical Approaches to Demonology,* Oxfordshire: Routledge, https://www.taylorfrancis.com/chapters/edit/10.4324/9781315466774-11/justified-belief-existence-demons-impossible-david-kyle-johnson (Accessed 10/14/2022).
[2] This is thoroughly documented in my 555 page anthology, *Christianity is not Great: Why Faith Fails* (Amherst, NY: Prometheus Books, 2014). See also Richard Carrier, "What's the Harm? Why Religious Belief Is Always Bad", *Richard Carrier Blogs,* https://www.richard-carrier.info/archives/14557 (Accessed 10/14/2022).
[3] See Plantinga, Alvin (2000) *Warranted Christian Belief* (Oxford: Oxford University Press), 2000.
[4] Craig, William Lane (1984), *Apologetics: An Introduction,* Chicago: Moody Press, pp. 18-22.

Craig says he *knows* Christianity is true not because of any historical evidence. He writes: [1]

> In considering the historical evidence for the resurrection of Je-
> sus, it is important to avoid giving the impression that the Christian faith
> is based on the evidence for Jesus' resurrection. The Christian faith is
> based on the event of the resurrection. It is not based on the evidence
> for the resurrection.
>
> This distinction is crucial.
>
> The Christian faith stands or falls on the event of the resurrection.
> If Jesus did not rise from the dead, then Christian is a myth, and we may
> as well forget it. But the Christian faith does not stand or fall on the evi-
> dence for the resurrection.

Craig explains:[2]

> If we insist on a historical, evidential foundation for faith, then we
> consign most of the world's population to unbelief. To me this is uncon-
> scionable. Therefore, if one's religious beliefs are to be rational, there
> must be some other basis for them than the evidence. We are therefore
> not dependent on historical proofs for knowledge of Christianity's truth.
> Rather through the immediate, inner witness of God's Holy Spirit every
> person can come to know the truth of the Gospel once he hears it.
> Through an existential encounter with God Himself every generation
> can be made contemporaneous with the first generation of believers.

Craig cites the Bible as the ultimate authority on this, concluding,[3]

> The Bible says all men are without excuse [Romans 1]. Even men
> who are given no good reason to believe and many persuasive reasons
> to disbelieve have no good excuse, because the ultimate reason they
> do not believe is that they have deliberately rejected God's Holy Spirit.
> Therefore, the role of reason in knowing Christianity is true is to be a
> servant. A person knows Christianity is true because the Holy Spirit tells

---

[1] Craig, *The Son Rises: The Historical Evidence for the Resurrection of Jesus* (Chicago: Moody Press, 1981): p. 7.
[2] "William Lane Craig's Answer To Lessing's Ugly Broad Ditch" at https://www.debunking-christianity.com/2022/07/william-lane-craigs-answer-to-lessings.html
[3] Craig, William Lane (1984), *Apologetics: An Introduction*, Chicago: Moody Press, p. 22. The Bible says it. That settles it, right?

him it is true, and while reason can be used to support this conclusion, reason cannot overrule it.

Therefore Craig concludes:[1]

> It is never an appropriate response to defeaters to abandon Christian faith and reject Jesus Christ and the witness of the Holy Spirit. Rather, God can be trusted in such circumstances where we feel at a loss as to how to answer the defeater and we have no extrinsic defeater of the defeater, God can be counted on to so intensify the witness of the Holy Spirit that that will enable us to have an intrinsic defeater-defeater so that the appropriate response is to continue to believe with the hope that someday we may, in fact, find an error in that defeater and be able to expose its falsehood. The witness of the Holy Spirit is an intrinsic defeater-defeater.

To see just how deep he goes, Craig says, "I am asserting that not only should I continue to have faith in God on the basis of the Spirit's witness even if all the arguments for His existence were refuted, but I should continue to have faith in God even in the face of objections which I cannot at that time answer."[2]

Craig is not alone. He stands in a long line of theologians, philosophers, and apologists who disparage evidential reasoning in favor of blind faith—the only kind of faith that exists. It begins with Jesus, who purportedly said, "I praise you, Father, Lord of heaven and earth, because you have hidden these things from the wise and learned, and revealed them to little children. Yes, Father, for this was your good pleasure." (Luke 10:21). Paul wrote, "The message of the cross is foolishness to those who are perishing, but to us who are being saved it is the power of God. For it is written: 'I will destroy the wisdom of the wise; the intelligence of the intelligent I will

---

[1] Craig, William Lane (2021), "An Objection to the Witness of the Holy Spirit", *Reasonable Faith,* April 19, 2021, https://www.reasonablefaith.org/media/reasonable-faith-podcast/an-objection-to-the-witness-of-the-holy-spirit (Accessed 14/10/2022). See also "Answering Critics of the Inner Witness of the Spirit", *Reasonable Faith,* August 17, 2014, https://www.reasonablefaith.org/media/reasonable-faith-podcast/answering-critics-of-the-inner-witness-of-the-spirit (Accessed 14/10/2022).
[2] Craig, William Lane (2009), "Question #136: The Witness of the Spirit as an Intrinsic Defeater-Defeater", *Reasonable Faith,* November 23, 2009, https://www.reasonablefaith.org/writings/question-answer/the-witness-of-the-spirit-as-an-intrinsic-defeater-defeater (Accessed 14/10/2022).

frustrate.' Where is the wise man? Where is the scholar? Where is the philosopher of this age? Has not God made foolish the wisdom of the world?. . . For the foolishness of God is wiser than man's wisdom" (1 Cor. 1:18–25). In Colossians 2:8 we read, "See no one takes you captive through hollow and deceptive philosophy." Tertullian (160–220 CE) asked: "What has Athens [the seat of philosophical reasoning] to do with Jerusalem [the seat of religious faith and theology]?" In words suggestive of philosopher Søren Kierkegaard, Tertullian wrote of the incarnation of Jesus by saying, "Just because it is absurd, it is to be believed . . . it is certain because it is impossible." Martin Luther called reason "the Devil's Whore." As such, reason "can do nothing but slander and harm all that God says and does." Immanuel Kant said that, "I have found it necessary to deny knowledge in order to make room for faith."[1]

There is something wrong with a religious faith that needs to disparage reason like this. It's admitting Christianity cannot be defended by reason. If that's so, why should anyone think otherwise? In fact, a great many Christian theologians don't think highly of apologetics. Following in the footsteps of Karl Barth, acknowledged as the greatest theologian of the last century—whom I wrote my M.A. master's thesis on—they think apologetics is a failure.[2] In their colleges, there is no apologetics department, or apologetics classes. They say, "God is his own witness. Only God can reveal God. Revelation from God can only come from God." Or, as Barth himself said, "the best apologetics is a good dogmatics."[3]

---

[1] Kant, *Critique of Pure Reason*, Bxxix-xxx, p. 29.
[2] In my anthology, "The Case against Miracles" (Hypatia Press, 2019), I wrote a chapter called "The Abject Failure of Christian Apologetics." In it I show how upwards to 80% of Christian apologists reject the requirement for evidence (i.e., Evidentialism) in favor of four other apologetical methods. The best explanation for why they've come up with different methods of defending their faith is because they themselves don't think the evidence is good enough.
[3] Barth, Karl (1963), *Table Talk*, ed. J. D. Godsey, Edinburgh and London: Oliver & Boyd, p. 62.

The Importance of Craig's Conversion Testimony

William Lane Craig has publicly shared his personal testimony of how he became a Christian on his website.[1] It basically tells us all that we need to know about Craig's approach to Christianity.

He wasn't raised in a church-going family, but when he became a teenager in the sixties, he started searching for something real, by asking questions, such as "Who am I?", "Why am I here?", and "Where am I going?" So he searched for answers by attending a Christian church. He didn't search for answers by attending a Muslim Mosque, nor a Jewish Synagogue, nor a Hindu Temple, because he was raised in a Christian culture that prejudicially set the limits of answers he would accept. At this church, all he saw with his young prudish and judgmental eyes were "a pack of hypocrites" who were "pretending to be something they're not."

Craig became very bitter and angry toward the people in that church, and arrived at the fallacious hasty generalization that "Nobody is really genuine." People were "all just a bunch of phonies" he says.

He became angry at his own hypocrisy, which is a religious guilt trip he placed on himself, that led him to falsely say, "I couldn't see any purpose to life; nothing really mattered." This is an unjustified either/or fallacious conclusion. There can be plenty of purposes and plenty of things that matter in one's daily life (like family, friends, and meaningful work), without needing one single final absolute unchanging purpose in life.

Then Craig met a girl. Her name was Sandy. She "always seemed so happy it just makes you sick!" he tells us. Upon asking Sandy why she was so happy, she told him "the God of the universe loved him and wanted to live in his heart." Sandy also introduced him to other Christians. Of them he said, "I had never met people like this! Whatever they said about Jesus, what was undeniable was that they were living life on a plane of reality that I didn't even dream existed, and it imparted a deep meaning and joy to their lives, which I craved."

Craig says that seeing happy people like this "hit me like a ton of bricks." The thought that the God of the universe really loved him "just staggered me." Continuing he said, "To think that the God of the universe should

---

[1] Craig, William Lane (2008), "Question #78 Personal Testimony of Faith", *Reasonable Faith*, on October 13, 2008, https://www.reasonablefaith.org/writings/question-answer/personal-testimony-of-faith (Accessed 15/10/2022).

love me, Bill Craig, that worm down there on that speck of dust called planet Earth! I just couldn't take it in." He recollects, [1]

> I thought to myself (and I'm not kidding) I thought if there is just one chance in a million that this is true it's worth believing...Far from raising the bar or the epistemic standard that Christianity must meet to be believed, I lower it. I think that this is a message which is so wonderful, so fantastic, that if there's any evidence that it's true then it's worth believing in, especially when you compare it to the alternatives like naturalism or atheism or other forms of life...When someone really knows what it's like to experience the love of God and to have this hope in eternal life and forgiveness of sins then it seems to me that he will gravitate toward that alternative. It will be so attractive and that it would take really, really decisive disproofs to make him give up his Christian faith and abandon it.

Craig then began a period of soul-searching for six months. He got a New Testament and read it from cover to cover—not the Koran, nor the Old Testament, nor any other religious, or non-religious text. Instead, he says, he read Christian books, attended Christian meetings, and sought the Christian god in prayer. That's how he investigated his faith. It was doing very poor research, even if his studies included the apologetics books available at the time by all the most famous and leading Christian apologists. Because reading apologetics books is not giving due diligence to an honest search for truth. If Craig had honestly and carefully investigated his faith, he should also have researched the major religious alternatives and considered their claims, and counter-arguments, including those of moderates, liberals, deists and non-believers.

Craig should have done what he would do when buying a brand new car: Do as much research as possible into the pros and cons of the intended purchase. There is no indication Craig did this with his religion, nor does he ever urge anyone else to do so. In fact he discourages doing so. [2]

[1] Craig, William Lane (2022), "Questions on Quantum Mechanics, Certainty, and Extreme Resistance", *Reasonable Faith*, July 18, 2022, https://www.reasonablefaith.org/media/reasonable-faith-podcast/questions-on-quantum-mechanics-certainty-and-extreme-resistance (Accessed 15/10/2022).
[2] Craig, William Lane (2013), "Question #340 Garbage In, Garbage Out", *Reasonable Faith*, October 21, 2013 https://www.reasonablefaith.org/writings/question-answer/garbage-in-garbage-out (Accessed 15/10/2022).

Finally, one night Craig came to the end of his rope and cried out to God. He subsequently "felt this tremendous infusion of joy!" Then he rushed outdoors, and as he looked up at the Milky Way galaxy of stars he thought, "God! I've come to know God!" That moment changed his whole life, he tells us. "Knowing God suddenly brought eternal significance to my life." That's when he decided he should spend his entire life spreading this same message. Many ex-Christians have known this same feeling. But one's feelings of exhilaration do not depend on whether such a story is objectively true, since feeling can mislead us into a false sense of undue certainty. Psychologist Valerie Tarico tells us, [1]

> The "feeling of knowing" (rightness, correctness, certainty, conviction) should be thought of as one of our primary emotions, like anger, pleasure, or fear. Like these other feelings, it can be triggered by a seizure or a drug or direct electrical stimulation of the brain. Once triggered for any reason, the feeling that something is right or real can be incredibly powerful—so powerful that when it goes head to head with logic or evidence the feeling wins. Our brains make up reasons to justify our feeling of knowing, rather than following logic to its logical conclusion. For many reasons, religious beliefs are usually undergirded by a strong "feeling of knowing." Set aside for the moment the question of whether those beliefs tap underlying realities. Conversion experiences can be intense, hypnotic, and transformative. Worship practices, music and religious architecture have been optimized over time to evoke right brain sensations of transcendence and euphoria. Social insularity protects a community consensus. Repetition of ideas reinforces a sense of conviction or certainty. Religious systems like Christianity that emphasize right belief have built in safeguards against contrary evidence, doubt, and the assertions of other religions.

For Craig, there was just one problem. At the end of his chapter on the problem of miracles, Craig confessed: "In my own case, the virgin birth was a stumbling block to my coming to faith—I simply could not believe such a thing. But when I reflected on the fact that God had created the entire universe, it occurred to me that it would not be too difficult for Him to make

---

[1] See Tarico, Valerie (2009), "Christian Belief Through the Lens of Cognitive Science: Part 3 of 6", "I Know Because I Know", *Debunking Christianity,* https://www.debunking-christianity.com/2009/06/christian-belief-through-lens-of.html (Accessed 10/16/2022).

a woman pregnant."[1] It appears as if Craig was reasoning himself into belief after all.

However, the young Craig reasoned poorly.

While he's correct that a creator god wouldn't have any trouble getting a virgin woman pregnant, that's not the problem. The problem is whether a creator god *really did that in this particular case* with the virgin Mary. Craig failed to take seriously the overwhelming objective evidence against such a miraculous claim. He also failed to grasp why the Jews of Jesus' day didn't believe the virgin birth tale, even though they were there, and believed in god, in Old Testament prophecy, and in miracles.[2]

We can learn some significant things from Craig's conversion testimony.

Craig was not *reasonably* converted into the faith he now defends. Happy people did the trick since he was an unhappy anxious teenager. It's pretty clear that the only religious faith he "investigated" was one sect within Western Protestant Christianity. He read the Christian New Testament allegedly produced by his Spirit Guide, who in turn confirmed it. That's like using the book allegedly produced by Allah to inform or educate us about the activity of Allah, who in turn confirms it.

Craig fallaciously believed the Christian story had more going for it than other religious stories, and that this was a good reason for him to believe. But almost every religion provides a purpose to life, a sense of importance in the grand scheme of things, an intimate awareness of a spirit world, a zest for life, relief from any real or imagined guilt, and an assurance of being saved from the drudgery of a mundane worldly existence in an immeasurable universe. They are also offered a deep sense of community and love by other believers.

By contrast, I can imagine a religious story that is much better, one with a god who loves and forgives us unconditionally as a perfect father would, with no punishment for any offenses, and with no need for an atonement so that everyone ends up in a blissful afterlife when they die. I can imagine a god placing us in a much better world than he has done too (see my anthology *God and Horrendous Suffering*). That being said, the specific

---

[1] Craig, William Lane (1984), *Apologetics: An Introduction*, Chicago: Moody Press, p. 125.
[2] See Case #2, "Christianity is Unworthy of Thinking Adults: Three Decisive Cases in Point", *Debunking Christianity*, https://www.debunking-christianity.com/2018/04/christianity-is-unworthy-of-thinking.html (Accessed 10/16/2022).

religious story told has little or nothing to do with whether or not that story is true. The only religious stories that count, if any of them do, are the ones having a sufficient amount of evidence for them. A story about a horrific god like *Whiro*: Evil God of Māori Mythology, or *Lilith*: Female Demon of Jewish Folklore, or *Loviatar*: Finnish Goddess of Death, Pain, and Disease, or *Apophis*: Evil God of Chaos in Ancient Egypt would be preferable *if the objective evidence led us to think so.*

The bedrock of Craig's faith is subjective, felt in the inner witness of a disembodied publicly undetectable Spirit Guide from "the other side." This is the basis for him *showing* his faith is true, even if he fails to *show* that it's true.

Mormonism and Craig

Doubt is the adult attitude, as I've argued.[1] But with Craig, there is no sense at which he thinks doubt is a virtue. It's not a reasonable option for him. He claims to have a Spirit Guide who assures him he's right. So he never expresses the fact that doubt is a means to get at the truth. He cannot urge Christians to doubt the inner witness of a Spirit Guide, since it's the basis for everything he believes.

Contrary to Craig, 17th-century French philosopher René Descartes argued by example that it is a good thing to doubt everything in order to see what he could legitimately accept afterwards (his *cogito ergo sum*). Descartes calls upon every adult to doubt as a means for honestly searching for truth: "If you would be a real seeker after truth, it is necessary that at least once in your life you doubt, as far as possible, all things." Craig did not do this. He doesn't recommend it.

Craig thinks he can special plead his way to his sect-specific Christianity because of his Spirit Guide. He can't legitimately do this. We just need to compare his Spirit Guide to the Spirit Guide of Mormon missionaries.

One of the chief defenders of Mormonism is Robert L. Millet, professor of ancient scripture and former dean of religious education at

---

[1] Loftus, John W. (2012), "Why Doubt Is The Adult Attitude And How Science Helps Us", *Debunking Christianity,* https://www.debunking-christianity.com/2012/06/why-doubt-is-adult-attitude-and-how.html (Accessed 10/16/2022).

Brigham Young University. Millet wrote a book called *Getting at the Truth: Responding to Difficult Questions about LDS Beliefs.*[1] He argues as Craig does, as if they were twins:

> In a very real sense believing is seeing. No member of the church need feel embarrassed at being unable to produce the Golden Plates or the complete Egyptian papyrus. No member of the church should hesitate to bear testimony of verities that remain in the realm of faith, that are seen only with the eyes of faith.
>
> In the end the only way that the things of God can be known is by the power of the Holy Ghost... the only way spiritual truth can be known is by the quiet whisperings of the Holy Ghost.
>
> I'm grateful to have, burning within my soul, a testimony that the father and the son appeared to Joseph Smith in the spring of 1820, and that the Church of Jesus Christ the Latter-Day Saints is truly the kingdom of God on Earth.

Millet then shares what other important Mormons have said:

> President Ezra Taft Benson: "We do not have to prove the Book of Mormon is true. The book is its own proof. All we need to do is read it and declare it.... *We are not required to prove that the Book of Mormon is true or is an authentic record through external evidences--though there are many. It never has been the case, nor is it so now, that the studies of the learned will prove the Book of Mormon true or false....*"
>
> President Gordon B. Hinckley, regarding the Book of Mormon: "The evidence for its truth, for its validity in a world that is prone to demand evidence lies not an archeology or anthropology, though these may be helpful to some. It lies not in word research or historical analysis, though these may be confirmatory. *The evidence for its truth and validity lies within the covers of the book itself.* The test of its truth lies in reading it. It is a book of God. Reasonable individuals may sincerely question its origins, but those who read it prayerfully may come to know by a power beyond their natural senses that it is true."

---

[1] All of the following quotes are from *Getting at the Truth* (Salt Lake City: Deseret Book Co., 2004), pp. 36-39, which are shared by Mark Mittleberg, *Confident Faith* (Carol Stream, IL: Tyndale House Publishers, 2013), pp. 106-8, Italics mine.

Craig advocates a duo approach to Christianity. On the one hand, his Spirit Guide is all he needs in order to *know* Christianity is true. But on the other hand, Craig says he can *show* reasons for his faith that confirm the inner witness of his Spirit Guide. Whether it's the Mormon Spirit Guide or the Book of Mormon given by the Spirit, this is what important Mormons also say.

So a very serious problem emerges. How can they dispute each other's Spirit Guide claims when their different faiths originate from self-attesting Spirit Guides, apart from any evidence or argument? Each of them denies the need for any evidence, so they cannot show the other Spirit Guide's witness is wrong by means of evidence. Doing so would deny their respective claims that the evidence isn't needed. All they can say is that their Spirit Guide testifies to their specific religion, which *de facto* denies each other's religion. So it's no surprise that this is exactly what Craig does when asked about the Mormon faith claim. "They are wrong" he asserts. "I'm right" he asserts. That's the end of the matter.[1]

It should be crystal clear that if two different Christianities (or religions) both reject the need for evidence, then claim to know their faith is the correct one based on a Spirit Guide who leads them into the truth (e.g., John 14:26; 15:26; John 16:13-14; 1 Corinthians 2:10-13; 1 John 2:27), something is seriously wrong. It reveals the sham of *Psychic Epistemology* as an apologetical ploy, because it justifies believing whatever one wants to believe, defeaters, both intrinsic and extrinsic be damned.[2] If it can lead believers to conflicting Christianities,[3] then a Spirit Guide from "the other side" should be rejected if one honestly desires to know which religion is true, if one is at all.

[1] Craig, William Lane (2010), "Q #167 Counterfeit Claims to the Witness of the Spirit", June 28, 2010, *Reasonable Faith*, https://www.reasonablefaith.org/writings/question-answer/counterfeit-claims-to-the-witness-of-the-spirit (Accessed 10/16/2022).
[2] For an introduction see Sudduth, Michael (n.d.), "Defeaters in Epistemology", *Internet Encyclopedia of Philosophy*, https://iep.utm.edu/defeaters-in-epistemology/ (Accessed 10/16/2022). Religionists should approach all defeaters to their respective faiths from the perspective of an outsider, a non-believer, as I argue in my book, *The Outsider Test for Faith*.
[3] I refuse to judge between believers who claim to be Christians. I accept whatever label they use, since it's just a label.

The Propositional Content Objection

The Mormon doctrinal difference is an egregious example of a fundamental problem. Let's highlight here the propositional content of *Spirit-Guided Epistemology*. Consider what Plantinga says. The Christian believer can be rational in knowing "God has created the world even if he has no argument at all for that conclusion,"[1] and in having a "full-blooded Christian belief"[2] in "the great truths of the gospel."[3]

Plantinga says:[4]

> [W]e don't require argument from, for example, historically established premises about the authorship and reliability of the bit of Scripture in question to the conclusion that the bit in question is in fact true; for belief in the great things of the gospel to be justified, rational, and warranted, no historical evidence and argument for the teaching in question, or for the veracity or reliability or divine character of Scripture are necessary.

Plantinga believes we all have a sense of divinity (or *sensus divinitatis*, if you prefer the Latin) within us, a (holy) Spirit Guide who gives witness to "the great truths of the gospel" when reading the Scripture. This is the same kind of thing psychics claim they can do by reading tea leaves and tarot cards. He's effectively saying the spirit world gives Christians these same kinds of psychic abilities.

Pay close attention to what Plantinga says. "Faith involves an explicitly cognitive element; it is, says Calvin, knowledge...and it is revealed to our minds. To have faith, therefore, is to know and hence believe something or other." And Christian beliefs come "by way of the work of the Holy Spirit, who gets us to accept, causes us to believe, these great truths of the gospel. These beliefs don't come just by way of the normal operation of our natural

---

[1] Plantinga in Plantinga, Alvin & Wolterstorff (eds.) (1983), Nicholas "Reason and Belief in God," in *Faith and Rationality: Reason and Belief in God*, Notre Dame: University of Notre Dame Press, p. 65.
[2] Plantinga, Alvin (2000), *Warranted Christian Belief*, New York: Oxford University Press, p. 200.
[3] Ibid., pp. 245, 262
[4] Ibid., p. 262.

faculties, they are a supernatural gift.[1] If this is not claiming to have psychic abilities, then I don't know what is.

Now take a look at the propositional content Craig proposes. He says his Spirit Guide "produces an awareness of the truths of the Gospel, assurance of salvation, conviction of sin, things of this sort." Based on it, he says "you can know that God exists and that Christianity is true wholly apart from arguments" and "know with confidence that Christianity is true...and the great truths of the Gospel are correct."[2]

Their Spirit Guide imparts a whole host of doctrines, which end up largely being the essentials of a whole religion, based on creedal affirmations by the dozens and dozens.[3] Every "essential" doctrine within Christian theology has been endlessly debated and some have even been fought over. Do Craig and Plantinga fail to realize that eight million Christians killed each other during the French Wars of Religion, and the Thirty Years War, over such things as the real presence of Christ in the Eucharist, and who was the legitimate authority to administer it? Where was the Spirit Guide?[4]

Look at the virgin birth again. What does Craig do with Christian disagreement here? In the *United States* according to a 1998 poll of 7,441 Protestant clergy, the following ministers said they didn't believe in the virgin birth:[5]

- American Lutherans, 19 percent
- American Baptists, 34 percent
- Episcopalians, 44 percent
- Presbyterians, 49 percent
- Methodists, 60 percent

[1] Ibid., pp. 245-246.
[2] Craig, William Lane (2009), "Religious Experience: Subjective or Objective?", *Reasonable Faith Podcast*, https://www.reasonablefaith.org/media/reasonable-faith-podcast/religious-experience-subjective-or-objective (Accessed 10/16/2022).
[3] Leith, John H. (ed.) (1982), *Creeds of the Churches, Third Edition: A Reader in Christian Doctrine from the Bible to the* Present, Louisville, KY: Westminster John Knox Press; 3rd edition. This 748 page-turner of a book offers, in one comprehensive book, the major Christian statements of faith from biblical times to the present,
[4] In a chapter written for *The Christian Delusion* (Amherst, NY: Prometheus Books, 2010) "What We've Got Here is a Failure to Communicate," I look at these doctrinal disputes, the results, and question the wisdom and care of the Spirit.
[5] Source for these statistics can be found in Unruh, Bob (2015), "'Fairy tale': Many pastors don't believe Jesus born of virgin," *WND*, https://www.wnd.com/2015/12/christian-preacher-nativity-story-just-fairy-tale/ (Accessed 10/17/2022).

In the *United Kingdom* a poll surveying 103 Roman Catholic priests, Anglican priests, and Protestant ministers found that "25 percent didn't believe in the virgin birth," while in *Scotland*, the state church found in a 2004 survey of ministers that "37 percent don't accept the virgin account."[1]

Apparently, Craig's Spirit Guide can convince other Christians to accept false doctrines, ones based on poor judgment, poor reasoning and/or poor evidence. Craig was right to question the tale of a virgin birthed son of a deity, as I have argued.[2] It never happened. That makes Craig's (holy) Spirit Guide ignorant of the facts, or okay with people believing on insufficient evidence based on poor reasoning. Or, at worst, the Holy Spirit is a liar.

So which view of how Jesus came into the world is the authentic Spirit Guide's version of Christianity? Which god and which Christianity is the Christian Spirit attesting to? We don't have to ask Craig. We know. He teaches a weekly Sunday School class at his home church, Johnson Ferry Baptist Church in Marietta, Georgia. It's a conservative Baptist church. So guess what? His Spirit Guide confirms his conservative Baptist Church's Creedal Statement of Faith, since he must accept it to teach his weekly Sunday School class.[3] It's what he means by "Christianity" even though there ain't no such thing as Christianity, only Christianities.[4] What Craig ends up saying is that his church denomination is the true one with the most truth to it, and that he knows this despite any argument and any evidence to the contrary. A more deluded belief cannot be found. There must be a Spirit Guide for each denomination and each sect.

---

[1] Ibid.
[2] Loftus, John W. (2020), "The Gateway to Doubting the Gospel Narratives Is The Virgin Birth Myth," *Debunking Christianity*, https://www.debunking-christianity.com/2020/06/the-gateway-to-doubting-gospel.html, (Accessed 10/17/2022).
[3] See "Beliefs and Values," *Johnson Ferry*, https://johnsonferry.org/default.aspx?page=4349, (Accessed 10/17/2022).
[4] See these blog posts of mine: *Debunking Christianity*, https://www.debunking-christianity.com/search?q=mere+christianity, (Accessed 10/17/2022).

Cognitive Biases Run Amuck

The bottom line is that William Lane Craig fails in searching for religious truth given the human propensity to fool ourselves. The first person he's deceiving is himself, and secondarily he's giving Christian believers permission to deceive *them*selves.[1] This makes Craig *himself* an unreliable guide to religious truth, despite all of his arguments, both philosophical and historical.[2]

Believers like Craig simply create their own religion, their own gospel, and their own God in their own image. A major psychological study has proven this very point.[3] Craig's Spirit Guide is used by others who identify as Christians to justify theologies that Craig would reject as illegitimate, heretical, unusual, and strange. If Craig's Spirit Guide is really doing this, he/she/it is justifying conflicting Christianities, some of whom have gone to war with each other over their faiths. The best explanation is that Craig's Spirit Guide is identical with his own inner subjective feelings, despite all his obfuscations and special pleadings.

Cognitive biases act on our brains just like viruses. They adversely affect the ability of our brains to honestly evaluate our religious cultural indoctrination. Cognitive biases are known for giving people permission to confirm their biases **despite the fact that they are false**. So we must bring our reptilian brains to heel by demanding sufficient objective evidence that would convince an *outsider*.

Confirmation Bias is the mother of all cognitive biases. It is the tendency to search for, interpret, favor, and recall information in a way that confirms or supports one's prior beliefs or values. People display this bias when they select information that supports their views, ignoring contrary information, or when they interpret ambiguous evidence as supporting their existing attitudes. The effect is strongest for desired outcomes, for

[1] Loftus, John W. (2022), "William Lane Craig Utterly Fails In Searching For Truth Given the Human Propensity To Fool Ourselves," *Debunking Christianity*, https://www.debunking-christianity.com/2022/08/william-lane-craig-utterly-fails-in.html, (Accessed 10/17/2022).
[2] Loftus, John W. (2022), "William Lane Craig Utterly Fails In Searching For Truth Given the Human Propensity To Fool Ourselves," *Debunking Christianity*, https://www.debunking-christianity.com/2022/08/william-lane-craig-utterly-fails-in.html, (Accessed 10/17/2022).
[3] Loftus, John W. (2011), "The Danger of Belief is Thinking You Believe What God Does," *Debunking Christianity*, https://www.debunking-christianity.com/2011/03/danger-of-belief-is-thinking-you.html, (Accessed 10/17/2022).

emotionally charged issues, and for deeply entrenched beliefs. We are in constant search of confirmation, hardly ever do we seek disconfirmation. We reject and dismiss out of hand what does not comport to existing beliefs, and easily embrace beliefs that do.

There are other relevant biases, like Anchoring Bias, Ingroup Bias, Belief Blind Spot Bias, Belief Bias Effect, Illusory Truth Effect, Agent Detection Bias, Objectivity Illusion Bias, the Ostrich effect, Hindsight Bias, and so on.

These biases lead us to reason fallaciously. Believers are susceptible to fallacies like *Tu Quoque* ("You Too" – appeal to hypocrisy, whataboutism), *Possibiliter Ergo Probabiliter* ("Possibly, Therefore Probably"), Straw Man/Person, Argument from Ignorance, Appeal to Popularity (Ad Populum), Equivocation, False Analogy, Post hoc ergo propter hoc (Latin for "after this, therefore because of this"), Cherry Picking, Hasty Generalization, Circular Reasoning, Red Herring, Non-Sequitur, and especially Special Pleading.

The only way to disarm the brain (yes, basically the only way), is to adopt the perspective of a nonbeliever, an outsider to our indoctrinated religious beliefs. Given the power of cultural indoctrination doing this will allow believers to be open-minded to the scientific evidence of the nature of nature, its workings, and its origins, which in turn will allow believers to question any religion that holds beliefs contrary to scientific findings. The highest authority is the consensus of scientists working in a given field of studies. The only way for a non-scientist to reject these findings is to await a new consensus from scientists working in the same field. More than anything else this perspective can help the brain avoid cognitive biases in the honest search for truth. It will help force the believer's brain to follow the objective evidence wherever it leads. Treat your own religion the way you treat all other religions, with no double-standards and no special pleadings. Assume your own religion has the burden of proof. See if your faith survives.[1] What do you have to lose? Craig is scared he'll lose everything he's worked for, which would discredit him as a person, so I don't expect him to give up on his faith. Perhaps what I write can help others though.

Plantinga and Craig are prime examples of what philosopher Stephen Law said: "Anything based on faith, no matter how ludicrous, can be

---

[1] See Loftus, John W. (2013), *The Outsider Test for Faith*, Amherst, NY: Prometheus Books.

made to be consistent with the available evidence, given a little patience and ingenuity."[1] Or as anthropology professor James T. Houk said: "Virtually anything and everything, no matter how absurd, inane, or ridiculous, has been believed or claimed to be true at one time or another by somebody, somewhere in the name of faith."[2]

Given the existence of world-wide religious diversity, even among different Christianities, Peter Boghossian tells the naked truth: "We are forced to conclude that a tremendous number of people are delusional. There is no other conclusion one can draw." He says, "The most charitable thing we can say about faith is that it's likely to be false."[3] No wonder Boghossian goes on to make a difference between sitting at the adult table from sitting at the children's table. People like Craig, no matter how highly he's regarded, or how brilliantly he uses empty rhetoric without substance, are not allowed at the adult table for discussion until they first disavow faith in a (holy) Spirit Guide as a means for knowing the truth about God, gods, goddesses, religion, and theology.

---

[1] Law, Stephen (2011), *Believing Bullshit: How Not to Get Sucked into an Intellectual Black Hole*, Amherst, NY: Prometheus Books, p. 75.
[2] Houk, James T. (2017), *The Illusion of Certainty*, Amherst, NY: Prometheus Books, p. 31.
[3] Boghossian in a recorded presentation ("Jesus, the Easter Bunny, and Other Delusions: Just Say No!"), embedded at *Debunking Christianity*: "Faith Based Belief Processes Are Unreliable," https://www.debunking-christianity.com/2012/04/peter-boghossian-faith-based-belief.html, (Accessed 10/17/2022).

Afterword

By David Madison, PhD Biblical Studies

A few years ago, I referred to John Loftus as a "force of nature," because of his energetic marshaling of evidence against Christianity—and that was *before* his most recent anthologies were published. There will come a time when this major world religion will be but a memory, thanks to the efforts of serious thinkers who have spoken and written to expose its flaws. These include, for example, in another era, Robert Ingersoll, and in our own, Christopher Hitchens, Richard Dawkins, and John Loftus, whose contribution is especially valuable because he was once a Christian minister himself.

Or maybe Christianity won't be a memory at all—similar to belief in Thor and Isis and Osiris—if humanity manages to snuff itself out. In the ashes, who will remember the Jesus worshippers? There are indeed fanatical Christians want to hasten the apocalypse, to initiate their god's kingdom on earth. According to Jesus-script in the gospels, there will be catastrophic suffering when this happens. It's been 77 years since a nuclear weapon was used against a civilian population, but the nuclear arsenals remain, as do humans motivated by aggression and territoriality, with their minds locked by ancient mythologies. It will take extraordinary effort to prevent Christian nationalists from demolishing democracy in America.

All the more reason, therefore, to maintain our efforts to dismantle this ancient mythology that has more than two billion followers worldwide, *and* apologists committed to its defense and preservation. What a predicament: we're trying to survive in this complex, dangerous modern world, but a religion that emerged two thousand years ago still holds so many in its grip. John Loftus has had the courage and patience to engage with its contemporary apologists, as this book demonstrates.

Please appreciate what is going on here! Three major superstitions were combined to create Christianity:

(1) Belief that, once upon a time, a tribal sky god identified his "chosen" people, whom he often himself condemned and terrified, as is described in such detail in the Old Testament. When this chosen people had

185

suffered at the hands of one conqueror after another, this god promised an "anointed one," a messiah who would intervene to set things right. The timing was never specified, although the apostle Paul and the author of Mark's gospel were sure it would be *soon*.

(2) After the destruction of the Jerusalem Temple in 70 CE, animal sacrifice—the flow of blood to satisfy the tribal deity—came to an abrupt end. What to do? Belief in one single, unique human sacrifice assumed the role that animal sacrifice had played, as we read in Mark 10:45, "For the Son of Man came not to be served but to serve and to give his life a ransom for many."

(3) One prominent theme in religions of the Ancient Near East was belief in dying-and-rising gods—and anyone who signed on could be guaranteed eternal life. Paul was convinced that Christ was *the one and only*: "...if you confess with your mouth that Jesus is Lord and believe in your heart that God raised him from the dead, you will be saved." (Romans 10:9) The author of Matthew's gospel created dramatic narrative to drive home the point that Jesus' resurrection had magical properties: many dead people emerged from their tombs on Easter morning and wandered around Jerusalem (Matt. 27:52-53).

Why is this blend of superstitions considered worthy of debate? If we were asked to debate the local storefront medium, astrologers, flat-earthers or Holocaust deniers, we would decline: who wants to give them a platform and waste precious time? But Loftus debates the apologists for these ancient superstitions—who ignore logic and reason, evidence and science—because Christianity is so dangerous in its modern form. It distracts people from understanding our world and the Cosmos as they actually are, and there's a colossal worldwide bureaucracy still pushing it. And oh, the irony: that bureaucracy is hopelessly fractured because Christians themselves cannot agree on the fundamentals of their faith!

Chapters 12 and 13—in Part 2: *A Deeper Incursion*—are Loftus' reflections on the size of the universe as revealed by science, and its implications for personal theism. This resonated with me especially. I grew up on the northern Indiana prairie, and was endlessly fascinated by the spectacular view of the night sky. From my teen years, I was locked onto the importance of the Bible, which pushed me toward seminary. Slowly but surely, however, information about the Cosmos penetrated my mind. Loftus does a formidable job explaining how theism—especially totalitarian monotheism—is undermined by what we now know about the universe. Early in my seminary career, I had an important *ah-ha moment*: I was stunned by the realization that, while humans have been wondering/speculating about gods for a few thousand years, there might be intelligent beings *out there* who have been researching the Cosmos for hundreds of thousands of years—maybe even far longer. And Christianity has defined its god in great detail without input from anyone *out there*. Can anything be more arrogant than that? What are the chances that we got it right? Loftus offers careful, thorough analysis of our speculations, carried out in isolation on our Pale Blue Dot.

Earth-bound theologies, generated by the human imagination for millennia, are not up to the task of explaining the Cosmos: *especially* theologies burdened with so much incoherence, as is overwhelmingly the case with Christianity. The books written and edited by John Loftus (the list is at the front of this volume) demonstrate so clearly that apologists are fighting a losing battle. But the eternal life gimmick—the intense emotional investment in escaping death—feeds their determination to maintain defense of ancient superstitions.

www.ingramcontent.com/pod-product-compliance
Lightning Source LLC
Chambersburg PA
CBHW071433090426
42737CB00011B/1648